THE STADIUM

THE
The Architecture
STADIUM
of Mass Sport

Edited by Michelle Provoost

NAI Publishers Rotterdam

Contents

Photo essays

The favourite stadium of...

Essays

Dance, discipline, density and death

Camiel van Winkel

Zeljo-Sarajevo 1-2

Chris Keulemans

Stadium fever

Marieke van Rooij

Sport and fashion

Pauline Terreehorst

Interviews

Foreword

Does sport have anything to do with architecture or culture? We have been able to answer this question in the affirmative for some time now, but crossing the threshold of a stadium was for a long time reserved for dedicated fans, who put up with the lack of comfort and safety. Over the last two decades, however, there has been a real boom in the construction of stadia of a completely different calibre, though this is not the only reason why we have turned our attention to this subject. This book and the exhibition it accompanies examine the stadium and sport in a sociological, cultural, economic and political context.

As with the architecture of objects such as bridges, tunnels and floodgates, or the architecture of industrial buildings, the architecture of sports facilities also has its own particular history. Stadium architecture has its own distinctive typologies, engineering techniques and programmatic requirements: the stadium as an architectonic and engineering masterpiece, as an aspect of urban development plans and the stimulus for the revitalization of a region, the stadium as an impulse for economic development. All these aspects can help the stadium fulfil an important multifunctional role for the surrounding area.

A high-quality stadium is an important factor in the competitive jostling between cities, and the architecture of the stadium reflects its greater significance. The status of the stadium is now comparable with that enjoyed by the museum during the 1980s: it has become an absolute must for every self-respecting town or city, and architects regard stadium projects as increasingly prestigious. The new stadia are also undergoing a development similar to that seen in museum architecture all over the world: it is more than just a place where sports events are held. The character of the stadium and the new users it attracts is the result of the whole entourage: souvenir stalls, shops, cinemas, cafés, bars, and so on. The whole family now accompanies the fanatic supporters.

Sport has become an unmissable element of our Western culture. In the Netherlands the leading sport is soccer, while in the United States and Asia one of the most popular sports is baseball. The culture of sport affects all our lives. Not just through our active participation in sport and its positive effect on our health, but most notably in the way that 'passive' participation in sport has developed, for example watching competitive events in the stadium or on television, wearing casual sports clothing for everyday activities, and so on.

Stadium design involves more than simple construction; rather it expresses the significance of sport in our culture, as well as in the cultures of other countries or regions. The history of stadium construction is thus not only interesting as a series of architectonic highlights, but also as a reflection of cultural and social developments. This publication provides an overview of the variety of contemporary stadia, and looks forward to future developments.

The Stadium. The Architecture of Mass Sport is being published in conjunction with an exhibition of the same name in the Netherlands Architecture Institute in summer 2000. The idea of examining the topic of sports facilities is not new, but was given new impetus by the selection of the city of Rotterdam to co-host the Euro 2000 European soccer championships. The final will be played in the wonderful Rotterdam stadium De Kuip (Brinkman and Van der Vlugt, 1936).

I would like to thank the people who have worked on this book and the exhibition with such dedication and enthusiasm.

Kristin Feireiss
Director of the Netherlands Architecture Institute

Introduction

Stadium construction in the twentieth century has been largely the preserve of engineers. However many superb structures this may have yielded, it has also led to an unnecessary restriction on the way we regard stadia. For a stadium is not just an engineering work but an expression of popular and sporting culture; it is a feat not just of construction but of design. Stadia are among a number of building types that wound up being categorized as utilitarian but which have recently renewed their ties with architecture. Hence the emphasis in this publication on the architectural and urban planning aspects of stadium construction. In addition, it seemed only natural that the Netherlands Architecture Institute should look at the stadium as an expression of a particular aspect of mass culture, namely sporting culture. After all, it is the fact that a stadium is built to accommodate crowds that distinguishes it from an vacant allotment in a residential neighbourhood; the crowd provides the technical and logistical complexity of the building task as well as the social and symbolic significance of a stadium. Rather than treating the stadium as an isolated object, therefore, we have looked at it as the condensation point of social, technical and spatial developments that influence the design of a stadium and are discernible in the resulting building.

There are also more topical reasons for focusing on stadium architecture. In recent times there has been an upsurge in stadium design as a result of several factors and developments which, while they are not confined to stadium construction, do help to explain the recent boom.

Safety

Although stadium disasters are by no means a recent phenomenon, a succession of tragic accidents involving high numbers of casualties (Heysel 1985, Hillsborough 1985, Johannesburg 1991, Guatemala 1996) prompted an exhaustive investigation into the ways in which stadium design might contribute to greater safety. In England the resulting Taylor Report contained a package of stringent safety recommendations that were to have a worldwide impact on soccer stadia via FIFA and UEFA regulations. One requirement was that all terraces be replaced by individual, vandal-proof seats. In other developments a 'ditch' was dug between playing field and stands to prevent groups of spectators from becoming trapped against the perimeter fencing and to allow stewards and police to circulate more freely. Evacuation logistics aimed at making it possible to clear a stadium completely in a matter of minutes became an important aspect of stadium design. All in all, these measures represented a considerable quantitative boost for stadium construction and renovation and a qualitative boost for technological innovation in stadium design.

'Sport is very much a part of the leisure industry.'
Rod Sheard, p. 49

'Without a Major League team and the stadium to match it, a city simply does not count.'
Marieke van Rooij, p.125

Media

The Olympic Games held in Berlin in 1936 were the first Games to receive large-scale, professional media coverage. Yet it was not until well after the Second World War that television started to have a negative effect on the number of stadium visitors. Even then, it was the stadia themselves that were largely to blame for dwindling attendance figures: while they were busily swelling to accommodate record numbers of spectators (200,000 at Maracana Stadium, Rio de Janeiro 1956), they were also becoming less comfortable and less congenial for those same spectators. Increasingly sophisticated television coverage made it possible for people to watch the match in the comfort of their own home surrounded by friends. The stadium had no choice but to pick up the challenge; unless it offered the public greater comfort and more activities, its days were numbered. Stadia were accordingly equipped with numerous public amenities and entertainment geared to offering people a day out with the family.

Nonetheless, the number of spectators in the stadium is only a fraction of the total number of people watching any given match. From a purely financial standpoint, stadia could be reduced to sealed, black boxes bristling with cameras focused on the playing field, but devoid of stands and public. It is the value attached (especially in America) to the stadium's social function as a meeting place that prevents stadium construction from moving in this direction. No doubt there is also a media aspect involved here: live spectators provide the necessary 'atmosphere', in the same way as a live studio audience supplies the requisite laughter and applause for TV talk shows.

The most recent development is the introduction of sophisticated media inside the stadium. Even now a section of the public watches the match on giant video boards rather than by looking directly at the pitch. Apart from images of the players, these screens display match statistics, action replays and commercials. The outlook for the future, as expressed here in various interviews with noted stadium designers, is further development in this direction.

Mass/individual

As a building designed to accommodate large groups of people, the stadium is a good reflection of the fluctuating relationship between crowd and individual. European stadia built in the early twentieth century were not used exclusively for sport as we know it today, with its emphasis on breaking records and winning gold medals. Sport was also closely allied with political and cultural ideas. This was true not only of the modern Olympic Games (revived in 1896) but also of variously inclined political movements, especially in Germany, France and Italy. Both the socialist and nationalist-socialist parties in Germany saw sport as a means of promoting community spirit and counteracting what was seen as the sterile emphasis on competition and the passive role of the public. In the 1920s and 1930s political groupings from across the ideological spectrum took to staging 'mass games' in stadia where the public participated in grandiose pageants. Such pathos-filled productions were a particular feature of 1930s Germany with the stadium, surrounded on all sides by stands, providing the ideal conditions for public participation. One example of a stand built especially for this purpose is the one around the Reichssportfeld in Berlin, part of the complex built for the 1936 Olympic Games. In a propaganda exercise brilliantly captured on film by Leni Riefenstahl, Adolf Hitler seized the opportunity offered by these Games to demonstrate to the world the superiority of the Aryan race and the Nazi regime.

After the war the symbiotic relationship between sport and politics largely evaporated. The increased leisure time, democratization and prosperity of the 1960s resulted in more and more people becoming personally involved in sport, both actively and passively. In line with the growing individualization that was manifesting itself on numerous social fronts, the experience of sport, too, was individualized. The choice of which sport to follow, which team to support and what clothing to wear while doing so are all aspects that express the personality and lifestyle of the individual. At the same time stadium design has served to curb the destructive force of the crowd as manifested in hooliganism and stadium disasters. The crowd has been fragmented and its potential for destruction neutralized by, among other things, giving individuals their own seat. The sense of community and club life have suffered accordingly.

In stadium design the focus on individuals is reflected in stands for particular target groups, in increased comfort and in attempts to attract different groups of supporters, visitors and families. Not that control has vanished altogether; it is simply exercised less conspicuously by means of closed circuit cameras and special passes. Indeed, the increased comfort goes hand in hand with increased control. The stadium is a public building and as such it is subject to the same rules as public space in general where there is also a trend towards inviting architecture combined with a high level of supervision.

'The Stade de France represented the official canonization of football.'
Casper van der Kruit, p. 112

'There is no false shame, least of all in a football stadium, where aggression is all in the game.'
Chris Keulemans, p. 91

'Wherever the crowd appears, windows and doors get smashed'
Elias Canetti, p. 16

Multifunctionality

A stadium that confines itself to hosting home team matches is used at best once a week. Obviously this is nowhere near enough to pay for the construction and maintenance of such an expensive structure. Since the 1960s, therefore, stadium managers have looked for ways of increasing their building's usage value by making it suitable for other sports and even for completely different activities like concerts, conventions, trade fairs, evangelical gatherings and so on. This in turn has entailed major technical innovations, in particular for the playing field and the roof. In 1965 the Astrodome (Houston, USA) showed the shape of things to come: it was completely roofed over and had a pitch of artificial grass (Astroturf), thereby making it suitable for many more activities besides sport. Instead of one day a week, the multifunctional stadium could be used hundreds of days a year for all kinds of events. The Astrodome was followed by a long line of stadia featuring a wide array of coverings, sliding roofs, pitches that could be raised or shifted sideways, plus such ancillary facilities as hotels, offices, theatres and shops. Yet despite the fact that the commercial exploitation of modern stadia is so wide-ranging and sport itself accounts for only a small fraction of total income, running a stadium remains problematical.

Urban revitalization

The Astrodome was an autonomous, out-of-town object. Since the 1980s, however, stadia have increasingly been used as a means of injecting new life into listless inner-urban areas, so much so that they have become a major factor of urban planning. Once again it was the United States that gave the lead. Post-war suburbanization had denuded American downtown areas not just of housing and shopping centres but also of sports stadia. With its Oriole Baseball Park in Baltimore (1982), HOK, an architectural practice specializing in sports architecture, set the tone for a succession of stadia aimed at revitalizing inner-city areas. It was hoped that the stadium, with its multiple functions and large crowds of visitors, would initiate a return of vitality to the city centre. This expectation imposed quite different demands on stadium design: unlike stadia built in the amorphous urban periphery, inner-city stadia had to fit in with a pre-existing context. From that moment, the stadium sitting beside the motorway exit in a sea of car-strewn asphalt, became a thing of the past. Henceforth a stadium was expected to merge programmatically and architecturally with its surroundings.

Postcard image

The stadium's new urban role also created the conditions whereby a city can identify with its stadium, regard it as a calling card or use it to trump rival cities in the struggle to attract tourism and business. The consequences of this are now also starting to filter through in Europe, where the St. Denis Stadium in France and the Amsterdam ArenA bear witness to a similar self-promotional strategy. The prestige now associated with stadium construction has resulted in growing dissatisfaction with existing stadia, many of them engineering works lacking in aesthetic pretensions. All of a sudden the stadium has become a prestigious design task for 'highbrow' architects of the likes of Peter Eisenman, Toyo Ito, Ben van Berkel or Kisho Kurokawa. We see here a parallel with other previously utilitarian design tasks like bridges and infrastructural works. Just as Ben van Berkel's Erasmus Bridge in Rotterdam symbolized the prestige of that city's 'leap southwards' or Frank Gehry's Guggenheim Museum put Bilbao on the world map, so stadium architecture is furnishing various cities with the desired postcard image.

Even when the setting is not an urban one, there is still a tendency to attempt to connect the building to its context, be it landscape, park or nature. Big sports complexes are broken up in accordance with local features; they seek to conform to the existing topography or even to merge with it altogether. The contextual approach has turned the stadium from autonomous object into a logical element of its surroundings.

Commerce

Sport's popularity and the attention lavished on it in all manner of media, mean that there is considerable commercial interest in sport and the venues where it is played. Sport has become big business. This is reflected in the players' clothing, bedecked and printed with logos, in the stadia, plastered with sponsors' signs, in the commercials that alternate with action replays on the giant video screens and, of course, in the stadium building itself. Since the 1980s, the corporate hospitality box has become one of the most profitable aspects of the stadium. The trend towards an ever-increasing percentage of such 'skyboxes' is demonstrated by the latest stadium in Lima, Peru, that boasts over 1,100 of these money-spinners. Restaurants and hotels with a view of the pitch are other attractions aimed at luring well-heeled supporters to the stadium. Naming rights, merchandising and concessions are the means by which the modern stadium generates its income.

'The *wave*, the telegenic symbol par excellence of the ironic crowd.'
Camiel van Winkel, p. 35

'The public experience of major sporting events no longer takes place in the stadium but in front of the television screen.'
Camiel van Winkel, p. 33

Sport has become one of the foremost leisure activities of our time, reaching into every corner of daily life. This is perhaps most clearly seen in the world of fashion where we find that not only has sports clothing has become normal daily wear, but that techniques and fabrics developed specially for sportsmen and women have also penetrated to the production of ordinary, ready-to-wear clothing. Sport has become a lifestyle: most Nikes are sold to people who never set foot on a playing field.

The Stadium. The Architecture of Mass Sport raises a number of themes relating to stadium architecture that have crystallized out in the course of the twentieth century: the shifting relationship between technology and design and thus between architect and engineer, the role of the architect in the complex process of building a stadium, the rise of architectural practices specializing in stadium construction, aspects of control, power and the abuse of stadia, the significance of the stadium as urban constituent, the various design attitudes to the image of the stadium, technological innovations, their origins and impact, the changing role of context, sporting culture and urban culture, and so on.

Given the large number of stadia built in recent years and scheduled to be built in the near future, this subject is one that will continue to command our attention in the coming years. The turbulent developments in sport, technology and the media have turned the stadium into a dynamic building type that is so susceptible to change that it is impossible to predict how it will look in twenty years' time.

The curators of the exhibition
'The Stadium. The Architecture of Mass Sport'
Matthijs Bouw
Michelle Provoost

'Outside, facing the city, the arena displays a lifeless wall; inside is a wall of people. The spectators turn their backs to the city. They have been lifted out of its structure of walls and streets and, for the duration of their time in the arena, they do not care about anything which happens there; they have left behind all their associations, rules and habits. Their remaining together in large numbers for the stated period of time is secure and their excitement has been promised them. But only under one definite condition: the discharge must take place inside the arena.'[1] Elias Canetti in *Crowds and power*

Dance, discipline, density and death

The crowd in the stadium

Camiel van Winkel

On 15 October 1936, three months after completion and five months before its inauguration, the Feyenoord Stadium in Rotterdam is subjected to a trial loading. Fifteen hundred marines and unemployed men file into a designated section of the stand. They stamp their feet on command and jump up and down in unison. Engineers measure the deformation of the suspended steel and concrete structure under their feet. Afterwards, the 'volunteers' are treated to a drink and a cigar.[2]

A photograph taken on this occasion, with the man who directed the crowd's movements via a megaphone in the foreground, serves to support the contention that the stadium, more than any other building type in the twentieth century, has been the scene of physical confrontation between crowd and architecture. When it comes to designing a stadium, architecture is synonymous with crowd control.

There is in the history of the modern sports stadium an ominous undercurrent of mutual provocation between crowd and architecture. The architecture attempts to impose discipline on the crowd, but time and again it transpires that designers and managers have miscalculated its blind force. Several major stadium disasters even pre-date the First World War. The worst of these took place in 1902 when a fifteen-metre high stand collapsed during a football international between Scotland and England at Ibrox Park, home of the Glasgow Rangers. In a crowd of 75,000 it was scarcely noticed how a group of several hundred fell through the planking and disappeared into the depths below. After a brief pause, the match continued. The final score was 1-1. The number of dead was twenty-six; 321 were seriously injured.[3]

The main function of a stadium is to accommodate the crowd; the occasion – whether it be a sporting or some other event – is secondary. If the destructive force of the crowd were simply a matter of cumulative weight, the problem of mass accommodation would have been solved back in the 1910s or 1920s. But a crowd entails more than static weight; its dynamic is determined by a combination of factors, such as density, movement, eagerness, expansion and panic. Load-bearing capacity alone is never sufficient to neutralize this explosive cocktail.

The events in the Hillsborough stadium in Sheffield on 15 April 1989 show that even at the end of the twentieth century the

Trial loading of the stand at Feyenoord Stadium in Rotterdam, 1936

logistics of the mass event could still go disastrously wrong. The final toll of ninety-six dead and a hundred and seventy injured was the consequence of a series of structural and incidental defects and mistakes in ticket distribution, police co-ordination and supervision, the capacity of entrance gates on the west side of the ground, the routing of supporters to the various enclosures, the spatial layout of the terraces and the cage-like structures used to keep supporters from invading the pitch. A sloping tunnel funnelled a surfeit of Liverpool fans into one of these 'pens'. At the very moment when this crush of people had become intolerable and the front rows were being pressed up against the steel perimeter fence, the police decided, in view of the huge influx of people and the chaos outside the ground, to throw open the exit gates as well.

Under the watching eyes of television cameras and irresolute stewards, hundreds

25 fans were killed and 517 injured when a stand collapsed at Ibrox Park Stadium in Glasgow, 1902

93 people were killed and 170 injured in the Hillsborough Stadium disaster in Sheffield, 15 April 1989

of supporters were squeezed together and dozens literally crushed. Eye-witness accounts from survivors of the crush give some idea of the immense physical forces at work within an enclosed crowd of people. 'From that moment on, I found myself pressed up against the person in front of me and both my arms were pinned between other people's bodies. That then meant that the only part of my own body that I was capable of moving was my head. Although my whole body was in severe discomfort, my left arm, left leg and back were in the most pain. In particular, a teenage girl who had been standing next to me had her head twisted round facing me, and the side of her face was being forced up against the upper part of my left arm. The excruciating pain in my arm was almost unbearable, and I feared that my arm was simply going to snap under the pressure. All I could see of the girl was her face, as the rest of her body was being smothered by other people. She was clearly in a great deal of pain. Her head was in a vice between my arm and the body of another man behind her. It was impossible for any of us to move at all. I could tell that the poor girl was having difficulty breathing and she was incapable of speaking, because her face was being squeezed so tightly that it was being contorted.' Another, female, supporter recalls: 'There was a bloke dying next to me. He was a really big bloke, like a docker. His mate was holding him up, trying to stop him from falling. The pushing from the back just forced you down. I was looking at the ground and thinking "If you go down there you're dead." The smell was unbelievable I can tell you. I was only at armpit level of most people because of my size. I was trying to force my head up in order to breathe. I remember shouting at the bloke next to me: "Move your arm, move your arm, you're killing me." I looked around and it was obvious that he was dead. His eyes, his tongue, I could tell.' A third: 'You can't recapture the sounds on television. You can hear a deafening hum, but you can't hear the person next to you screaming in your ear and you can't hear people dying and you can't hear bones crushing and you can't smell the smells. You could smell people dying.'[4]

Quotations such as these suggest that it would not be inappropriate to imagine the crowd as a living organism, an organism with a will of its own and a dynamism impervious to individual influence. As such, panic

lurks just below the surface in every crowd of people. Elias Canetti has described panic as the disintegration of the crowd from within the crowd.[5] An outbreak of panic in

same as himself. He feels him as he feels himself. Suddenly it is as though everything were happening in one and the same body.

Disaster in the Heysel Stadium in Brussels, 29 May 1985

a crowd amounts to a sudden return of the individual's fear of touch from which the crowd had temporarily released them.

It is the fundamental repugnance to being touched by someone or something unknown that, according to Canetti, is at the root of the distances and hierarchies that human beings have created around themselves.[6] 'It is only in the crowd that man can become free of this fear of being touched. That is the only situation in which the fear changes into its opposite. The crowd he needs is the dense crowd, in which body is pressed to body; a crowd, too, whose psychical constitution is also dense, or compact, so that he no longer notices who it is that presses against him. As soon as a man has surrendered himself to the crowd, he ceases to fear its touch. Ideally, all are equal there; no distinctions count, not even that of sex. The man pressed against him is the

This is perhaps one of the reasons why a crowd seeks to close in on itself: it wants to rid each individual as completely as possible of the fear of being touched. The more fiercely people press together, the more certain they feel that they do not fear each other. This reversal of the fear of being touched belongs to the nature of crowds.'[7]

The stories from the Hillsborough stadium make clear, however, that where there is increasing density and a lack of escape routes, sooner or later a second transition point will be reached, a point at which the suppressed fear of touch returns with added force, like a fatally delayed memory. Psychologically, the crowd disintegrates into a collection of individuals, although there can of course be no question of actual physical disintegration. The body of the crowd does not disintegrate until bones have been broken.

The Sheffield disaster, however appalling it may have been, was neither unique nor exceptional. The history of twentieth-century mass sport in Europe and beyond is littered with identical or comparable incidents. The role played by hooligans in the creation of these mass graves is virtually negligible. Many incidents involved a crowd pouring into a stadium too small to accommodate it or with inadequate stand access, so that the crowd literally trampled itself underfoot. This occurred in the English city of Bolton (1946, 33 dead), in Scottish Sutherland (1964, 2 dead), in the South-Korean city of Kwangju (1965, 14 dead), in Bukavu, Congo (1969, 27 dead), in Cairo (1947, 49 dead) and as recently as 1996 in Guatemala City (84 dead). Equally common is the reverse phenomenon: spectators inside a stadium panic and stampede towards the exit. Such exit panics have occurred in Buenos Aires (1944, 8 dead), in Jalapa, Mexico (1964, 24 dead), in Lima (1964, over 300 dead) and in Glasgow (1971, 66 dead). The panic may be prompted by riots (Buenos Aires, 1968, 73 dead; Brussels, 1985, 39 dead), a false alarm (Teresina, Brazil, 1973, 4 dead) or a sudden hailstorm (Kathmandu, 1988, 80 dead). 'Gurgling noises' emanating from a soft drink dispenser triggered a panic reaction among visitors to the Roosevelt Racecourse in Westbury, New York, in 1971, leading to 37 injured. The illusion that the stadium is about to collapse (Salvador, Brazil, 1971, 3 dead) can generate a panic every bit as real as the actual collapse of a wall (Sheffield, 1914, 75 injured) or a roof (Lille, 1946, hundreds trapped). And a goal in the final moments of a football match can result in a clash between a departing tide and groups of supporters who suddenly decide to turn around and go back to their seats (Moscow, 1982, 20 deaths).[8]

According to Canetti's theory, there exists a deep-rooted antagonism between crowd and architecture. It is in the nature of a crowd to want to grow. Buildings are like containers – 'pre-existing vessels'[9] – that limit the crowd's growth. Wherever the crowd appears, windows and doors get smashed: the dynamism of the crowd manifests itself as a collective destructiveness directed at all spatial boundaries and constraints. Underlying the smashing of windows and doors is a desire to fetch those who shut themselves away from the crowd out of

Casualties in the Burnden Park Stadium in Bolton, 1946

their houses, so that they may join it. 'In the crowd the individual feels that he is transcending the limits of his own person. He has a sense of relief, for the distances are removed which used to throw him back on himself and shut him in. With the lifting of these burdens of distance he feels free; his freedom is the crossing of these boundaries. He wants what is happening to him to happen to others too; and he expects it to happen to them.'[10]

Canetti distinguishes between open and closed crowds. The open crowd surrenders unhesitatingly to its natural urge to grow. It does not recognize 'houses, doors or locks'.[11] The open crowd expands in every direction, over streets and squares, and offsets the ever-present risk of disintegration by wholesale assimilation of individual elements. The closed crowd on the other hand reaches a compromise: it postpones growth and accepts spatial circumscription in return for permanence and repetition. The closed crowd knows that it is safe from external threats. The moment of discharge – 'the moment when all who belong to the crowd get rid of their differences and feel equal' – can be deferred and delayed because the crowd is certain of it.[12] Hence, the closed crowd in the stadium is characterized by a degree of stagnation. 'Its state has something passive in it; it waits.'[13] It savours and prolongs the phase of maximum density that precedes the discharge. The

physical sensation of being pressed together serves as a measure of the force of the collective organism. 'The more people who flow into that formation, the stronger the pressure becomes; feet have nowhere to move, arms are pinned down and only heads remain free, to see and to hear; every impulse is passed directly from body to body. ... This kind of density allows itself time; its effects are constant over a certain period; it is amorphous and not subject to a practised and familiar rhythm. For a long time nothing happens, but the desire for action accumulates and increases until it bursts forth with enhanced violence.'[14]

The crowd in the stadium submits patiently to the formulas and structures of mass accommodation. Although a sudden 'eruption' – a deliberate transition from a closed to an open condition[15] – always remains a possibility, the list of twentieth-century stadium disasters demonstrates how passively the closed crowd undergoes its manipulation in 'pre-existing vessels'.

In spite of the destructive reality of the antagonism between crowd and architecture, architects of the modern movement were forever playing with the crowd. It is no accident that Le Corbusier began his treatise Vers une Architecture (1923) with a series of pictures of grain silos – 'pre-existing vessels' par excellence – while Canetti mentions that same grain in his enumeration of the principal 'crowd symbols'.[16] After 1945, bulk technology became a standard point of reference in stadium design, as will be seen in the final part of this essay.

On this point it will suffice to draw attention to a curious duality in the architecture of the modern movement. On the one hand it engaged in a passionate flirtation with mass culture, mass media and mass transport; on the other hand, when it came to designing mass facilities it tended to disavow the weight of the crowd. The aesthetic rhetoric of modern architecture was all about lightness, transparency, immateriality, exposed supporting structures and slimmed-down structural elements. The Feyenoord Stadium in Rotterdam was the most extreme elaboration of such a rhetoric in stadium design: it consisted entirely of a slender, fine-meshed steel construction 'that would never have got building permission today'.[17] That this stadium in particular should have been subjected to a test load in the shape of fifteen hundred men seems like a perverse demonstration of self-confidence.

The cultic crowd

In parallel with its professionalization and breakthrough as a mass phenomenon in the 1920s and 1930s, modern sporting practice also emerged as a factor in the thinking of European cultural critics and intellectuals. The various ideological camps attributed cultural connotations to the phenomenon of sport; connotations that, whether positive or negative, were embedded in a broader vision of civic society in the interwar years.[18] Romantically inclined conservatives like Huizinga and Ortega y Gasset defended 'play' as the expressive core of human creativity and objected to what they saw as the trivialization and mechanization of this principle in contemporary sport.[19] Revolutionary ideologists of a fascist, socialist or communist disposition claimed that sport – together with other forms of public activity – had been depoliticized by bourgeois politicians for their own ends; they themselves aspired to renewed political colonization.[20] And a sceptically-minded intellectual like the novelist and one-time athlete Robert Musil, suggested that spiritual life had reahed an all-time low when a trained athletic body could be regarded as the acme of beauty and sagacity.[21]

In the intellectual arena of the interwar years, two 'stultifying' aspects of sport in particular were the subject of discussion: the one-sided emphasis on (record-breaking)

'Festspielstätte' design drawing by Johannes Seiffert, 1928

performance and the passive role of the public. The overblown spectacle of mass sport was the subject of widespread criticism in this period, from progressive and conservative observers alike. At the root of this criticism lay an aversion to the masses who were seen as stupid, barbaric, easily manipulated and shallow.[22] For their part, fascism, socialism and communism tried to bind the amorphous masses to their cause and to turn them into a disciplined 'movement'. This movement was supposed to create a new sense of community to compensate for the socio-economic processes that had alienated man from his true nature in the modern era. In their struggle against the liberal, individualistic model of society, the mass movements competed among themselves to offer the most attractive form of communal life. This resulted, among other things, in cult-like mass ceremonies and pageants that, despite their different ideological backgrounds, can to some extent be regarded as identical and interchangeable.[23]

These developments left their mark on stadium design in the 1920s and 1930s. The German architect and teacher Johannes Seiffert, who in 1928 published a treatise on facilities for sport and spectacle (Anlagen für Sport und Spiel), based his design studies on a cultural philosophy akin to National Socialism. His main premise was that sport (Kampfspiel) should be integrated with 'festive play' (Festspiel). The festival was the social rhythm of life in which the joyful harmonies of culture unfolded. In the course of such activities the mind learned to impart rhythm and emphasis to physical exercise, enabling the body to break free of its innate tendencies. According to Seiffert, a denial of the essence of play would lead irrevocably to cultural decline and warped ambitions. The new culture of the will should be borne on the wings of an original cult lest it waste away and be lost in mere Recordsiegen (record winning). In an age of argumentative intellectualism such a cult was to consist of a wordless 'service of becoming' (Werdensdienst) that transcended verbal argument and discord. For the consecration of play one could draw on those forms of art that were closest to the human body – singing and music – in order that the joy of competition might also be artistic joy. To counteract the materialistic pageantry of modern sporting events, Seiffert thought it essential that the Werdensdienst should be rhythmically structured by means of a prologue (march), celebration, competition and Ausklang (finale). The spatial framework should help to enforce harmony and rhythm. It was up to the designer of sporting accommodation to provide the Festraum (festive space) with a cultic focus so that spectators, too, might feel actively involved in the festive play. In the Festraum, the laws of space and the laws of play worked together to produce the all-embracing artwork of the festival. The festival contributed to the education of the people and their formation into a harmonious whole ('ein maßfreudiges Wir') – it helped prevent the 'Volk' from reverting to a 'horde'.[24]

In a number of design studies for Festspielstätten (festival venues) Seiffert translated these ideas into architecture. The cultic focus of his neo-classic sporting facilities consisted in each case of a choir stand placed in the open side of a horse-shoe shaped amphitheatre. 'Aufmarsch- und Übungsplätze' (parade and exercise grounds) were arranged symmetrically outside the actual stadium; ceremonial parades and processions could enter the playing field via wide aisles on either side of the choir. The result, judged by today's standards, was a hybrid amalgam of a sports arena and an open-air theatre. His biggest project was a 50,000 capacity Festspielstätte for national and international games. This design provided for a 'choir stand for musical and vocal opening and closing ceremonies', with space for a 300-piece orchestra and a 1,000-member choir. The roof of the main stand was specially designed to amplify the sounds and prevent them from being blown away.[25]

Although Seiffert drew his inspiration from the cultic games of ancient Olympia, where art, sport and religion were still organically interrelated, his approach struck a highly topical chord in 1920s Europe where stadia were routinely used for mass political gatherings designed to forge much the same mystical sense of community as Seiffert's Festspiele. The same period saw the emergence of a new, interdisciplinary form of theatre that was also performed in stadia. In Germany both developments converged in the National Socialist Thingspiele (pagan plays) of the years 1933-37.[26]

The political climate favourable to this radical reform of the theatre that arose in 1933 may have been ideologically coloured by National Socialism, but the momentum for reform came as much from the political left as from the right. Dissatisfaction with the traditional playhouse drama (perceived as ossified and middle-class) was widespread, and it was Bertolt Brecht who in 1926 had identified the sports audience as his ideal for the theatre: 'Our hopes are pinned on the sports audience. Our glance slides, let's not attempt to hide it, to these gigantic

cement pots filled with 15,000 people of every class and facial cast, the cleverest and fairest audience in the world ... The old theatre, on the other hand, no longer has a face.'[27] In practice, the anti-liberal, anti-individualistic orientation of the ideologies behind the Thingspiel movement partially coincided with the ideas of avant-garde reformers like Brecht.

An early source for the new theatrical spatial structure was the open-air theatre movement that arose around 1900.[28] The first Festspiele took place after the 1914-18 war under the auspices of organized working-class culture, in particular the annual 'Leipziger Massenspiele' (1920-24). With the aid of mass choreographies, choruses, choirs and dramatic tableaux backed up by musical and light effects, these mass performances presented the class struggle in historical and allegorical form. The production of Spartacus staged in the Leipzig velodrome in 1920 involved a cast of 900 and played to an audience of 50,000. The performance took place on a gigantic stage from where it spread out to occupy the entire stadium arena. Two years later the number of singers, dancers, actors and extras had risen to 3,000 resulting in a corresponding increase in the massiveness of the spectacle as a whole.[29] This massiveness was seen by contemporaries as an important cultural and political breakthrough: the intimacy of the elitist theatre had been thrown open to a new audience that included the proletariat. A reviewer wrote in 1923: 'Here the narrow space of the theatre or auditorium widens into a gigantic hall or the walls fall and the heavens provide the roof, with nature or the city as backdrop. Here the actors are proletarians, fresh from the lathe or the typing room. Here speak poets who have completely absorbed the struggles of the proletariat. Here poets, actors and spectators are united in one big community of experience.'[30]

From 1925 onwards, the mass spectacles of the socialist labour movement were held within the context of major gymnastic and sporting events. Thus, the first international working-class olympiad held in Frankfurt am Main in 1925 opened in cultic fashion with a Weihespiel (dedicatory pageant) entitled Kampf um die Erde (Battle for the Earth), written by Alfred Auerbach. The dramatic-historical line of this piece, which unfolded with much pathos and symbolism, linked the rebirth of the Olympic tradition to the dawning of the final phase of the international class struggle; sport

was thus assigned immediate relevance as a source of strength in the battle against oppression and injustice.[31]

The propensity for dramatization that characterized European politics in the 1920s was also evident on other fronts – for example in the organized Wechselreden (verbal exchanges) between leaders of paramilitary youth organizations and their followers; in the Kollektivreferaten (collective declamations) and works for chorus in support of the German communist party; and later in the large-scale choreographies with flags, floodlights and choruses staged during Nazi party rallies.[32] One can in fact speak of a new, externalized style of politics – often conducted in stadia – adopted by both ends of the ideological spectrum. 'Procession, march and battle song, verbal exchange between Führer and masses, rhythmically moving mass formations, uniform and salute, flag cult and symbol suddenly came together on the politicized street as on the open-air field turned stage.'[33] The crisis in the liberal system manifested itself in the parties' ambition to mobilize the masses; and the enormous scale of communication in the political arena demanded the deployment of uniforms, flags and other powerful visual aids, especially since they made it possible to play out the antagonism between the different movements in rhetorical fashion.[34] The tendency to view the disciplining of the masses as a prime political goal culminated in the programmatic vacuity of the National Socialists for whom spectacular mass choreographies took the place of ideological tracts and manifestos. The suggestion of unity, willpower and drive was a goal in itself; the slogans used by the Nazis – 'the release', 'the people', 'the national community' – were deliberately general and vague. This formalization of politics, which was carried out even more explicitly by the fascist parties in France and Italy, had the effect of a radical nationalization of inner life.[35]

In order to mobilize the masses it was essential to remove the distinction between participants and spectators at political events. This aim coincided with the desire of theatrical reformers to include the audience in the dramatic structure of the performance. Following Hitler's election victory and assumption of power in 1933, these reformers were given a free run in Germany and thus began the short but intense efflorescence of the nationalistic Thingspiel movement, the movement that would also constitute the

Free-style gymnastics in the stadium, Berlin Olympics, 1936

climax of the tradition of mass spectacles, Festspiele and Weihespiele of the previous decade.

The Thingspiel had the qualities of an eclectic Gesamtkunstwerk, combining elements of oratorio, pantomime, gymnastics, dramatic and balletic chorus, choral dance, flag parade, opera and military march. The psychologizing naturalism of the middle-class playhouse drama was exchanged for an abstract and allegorical representation of people and events. The subject matter was drawn from a mysticized, collective past. The ideal Thingspiel took the form of a historic duel in which the proto-Germanic community was confronted with an obscure or even diabolical opposing force. The dramatic structure of this confrontation was modelled on the Teutonic people's assembly or Thing, whereby the audience, in the role of 'the people who assemble', was actively

involved in the performance. This participation was further translated into spatial terms by having a chorus or groups of players move about the stands and among the audience.[36]

The first Thingspiele were written for stadium venues. On 1 October 1933 Berlin's Grünewald Stadium served as an open-air theatre for a performance of Brot und Eisen (Bread and Iron). The spectators numbered 60,000; the performers – members of the SA, policemen and soldiers, all in uniform – a staggering 17,000.[37] There were several reasons why stadia were considered suitable for these mass productions: their huge capacity meant they could accommodate the largest of spectacles; their openness made it possible to incorporate elements of the landscape into the drama; and the absence of proscenium, curtain and wings were instrumental in abolishing the one-dimen-

sional perspective of the traditional 'peep-show'.[38] In the stadium players and spectators shared one and the same dramatic-expressive space. The author of Brot und Eisen had this to say about it: 'That it was impossible to apply the dramaturgic rules of the Guckkastenbühne here was obvious; there was no apron, no curtain, no wings, only surface and space, a surface designed to be filled and divided up by rhythmically moving crowds, and a space that could never be dominated by the natural voice of the performer!'[39]

It was the multidimensional space of the sports arena, with stands on all sides, that served as a model for the specially designed Thingstätte (Thingspiel venues), the first of which was completed in July 1934. The largest, most prestigious and also the last to be built was the Dietrich-Eckart-Bühne in Berlin, part of the Reich Sports

Field constructed for the
1936 Olympic Games.[40]

The Functional crowd

Against the cultic approach to the stadium
as mass accommodation there is the functional and rationalistic approach. Although
they may at first glance appear to have very
little in common, both approaches reached
their euphoric zenith in the 1930s.

The interwar years found architects
gradually feeling their way towards the
ideal type of the modern sports stadium. In
this trial-and-error phase, which preceded
the post-war standardization of the typology,
two lines of development converged, both
of which had had their point of departure
in the nineteenth century.

The dual Greco-Roman model for
mass accommodation (amphitheatre and
hippodrome) was initially adapted to modern
sporting practice in a fairly intuitive way.
The chief impetus for this process was the
Olympic movement under the leadership of
Pierre de Coubertin.[41] When this French
baron embarked on his campaign to revive
the Olympic Games in 1892, there was no
such thing as an 'athletic stadium' anywhere
in the world. Consequently, for the first
modern Olympic Games held in Athens in
1896, the organizers reconstructed the
excavated hippodrome of Herodes Atticus
on a site near the Acropolis. During the
course of the Games, however, this marble
antiquity proved to be totally unsuitable as
a modern athletic facility: the oblong running
track was so narrow that runners were forced
to slow down in order to negotiate the sharp
bends. In addition, the infield was too cramped
to do justice to the various athletic events.[42]

The second problem requiring a solution
in this period had begun as a quite separate
issue: the need to open up the nineteenth-
century 'sports park' – typologically a sub-
group of the park – to a growing mass
public. The design of such municipal sports
parks was usually entrusted to landscape
architects or gardeners; a 'real' architect
was only brought in when a (tall) grandstand or a building containing ancillary
amenities was required. Examples of such
expanded complexes with dual designers
are the Frankfurt am Main sports park
(1922-25)[43] and the one on the Zeppelinfeld
in Nuremberg (1927-29). In the case of
Nuremberg the architect, Otto Ernst Schweizer,
was not called in until construction of the
park, designed by the municipal parks
department, had already begun. Schweizer

Sports park in Frankfurt, 1922-1925
Stand at the Vienna Stadium to a design by Otto Ernst Schweizer, 1928-1931
Stand at Nuremberg sports park to a design by Otto Ernst Schweizer, 1929

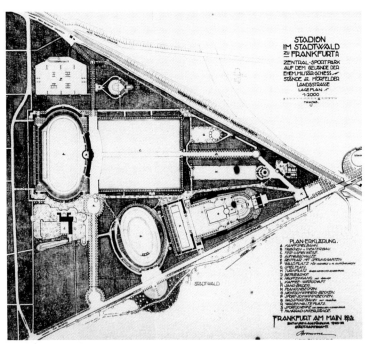

Olympic Stadium in Athens, 1896

Olympic Stadium in London, 1908
World's Fair Stadium in Turin, 1911

was given the difficult task of designing a grandstand, offices, shower and changing rooms, a café and a restaurant and fitting them spatially and logistically into the given park design.[44]

Only when the realization dawned that in certain circumstances it might make sense to combine these two design issues – the modernization of the classic stadium type and the opening up of the sports park to the masses – and to treat them as a single task, did a large-scale functional solution come within reach. That solution consisted quite simply of placing a compact stadium in a spacious sports park. By housing athletics and no more than one field sport (usually football) inside the stadium and arranging all other facilities (such as a velodrome, swimming pool and racecourse) around the stadium in a park-like setting, it was possible to achieve the proper balance between intimacy and massiveness, between surface area and structural volume, between public enjoyment and efficient circulation.

This solution, which had its first convincing elaboration in the Reich Sports Field built for the 1936 Berlin Games and which retained its popularity over the course of the century, seems so obvious now that it is difficult to imagine how stubbornly people in the early decades of the century persisted in trying to do the very opposite: namely, to bring the sports park inside the stadium.

At the London Olympic Games in 1908, for example, all sporting events were held in a single vast stadium for 80,000 people. Measuring 180 by 305 metres, the Shepherd's Bush Stadium comprised a football pitch, a cement cycling track, an athletics track and a 16 by 100 metres swimming pool; the archery contests were also held here along with the equestrian events.[45] The vastness of the site meant that a lot of the contests must have been missed by a lot of the audience. But there were even worse examples: the stadium built for the Turin World's Fair three years later covered 85 hectares (220 by 390 metres) and contained not only a cycling track and an athletics track but a racecourse as well.[46]

The slow progress of the trial-and-error design of large-scale stadia was once again in evidence at the Amsterdam Olympics (1928). The fact that a cycling track is bound, by virtue of its steeply banked corners, to cut into the stand area, thereby reducing seating capacity and lengthening sight lines, did not prevent the organizers from opting once

again (but now for the last time in the history of the Olympic Games) for a cycling track inside the athletics stadium.[47] When the inadequate stand capacity led to an enlargement operation in the 1930s, the architect, Jan Wils, had no option but to raise the height of those very end stands where the sight lines were already extremely long.[48]

The length of the athletics track in Wils's Olympic Stadium – 400 metres – was subsequently adopted as the international standard. In previous Games the length had fluctuated somewhat: 333 metres (Athens 1896), 500 metres (Paris 1900), 536

metres (St. Louis 1904, London 1908) and 382 metres (Stockholm 1912). The fact was that the rationalization of stadium design could not really begin until the umbrella sports organizations, convinced of the importance of international competition and comparative performance, had fixed these and other standard measurements.[49]

The stylistic high points of an integrated and 'functional' stadium architecture consequently date from the 1930s: Schweizer's stadium in Prater Park, Vienna (1931), Nervi's Stadio Communale in Florence (1932) and the Feyenoord Stadium by Brinkman & Van der Vlugt in Rotterdam (1936). These build-

ings also mark the period of the most direct
and thus also most naive confrontation between crowd and architecture. While Pier
Luigi Nervi still gave his Stadio Communale
a symbolic beacon in the form of a tower
inspired by the Marathon Tower at the
Amsterdam Olympic Stadium, the stadia in
Vienna and Rotterdam allowed the crowd to
manifest itself as a naked, purely biological
entity, stripped of all 'transcendental theories
and goals'.[50] The untreated concrete of the
one is just as bare and direct as the steel
trusses of the other. In both cases, the choice
of a quick and cheap production process
went hand in hand with an ingenious logistical
organization featuring a large number of
stand access points at different levels around
the stadium. Both facilities were renowned
for their exceptionally short evacuation
times: 7.5 minutes in Vienna,[51] 6 minutes
in Rotterdam.[52] At the same time, both
Schweizer and Van der Vlugt managed to
double capacity compared with the stadia
in Florence and Amsterdam: the first by
opting for 80% standing room, the second
by designing an all-round, double-decker
stand.

The Feyenoord Stadium was one of
the earliest examples of a mass facility to
have freed itself convincingly from the classic
model. The compact soapbox surrounded
by multi-level, cantilevered grandstands
was to become an important basic model
after the Second World War because it gave
all spectators an uninterrupted view and a

position relatively close to the playing field.
The object quality of the Rotterdam stadium,
which appeared as an autonomous, quasi-
industrial structure dropped into the otherwise empty polder, similarly anticipated
post-war trends.

Otto Schweizer, on the other hand,
had actually based his design for the Vienna
stadium on a detailed analysis of the Greco-
Roman arena; this analysis was, however, of
a purely functional nature, aimed at discovering the most efficient method of stand
access and the optimal dimensions for the
stadium space in relation to human vision.
Notwithstanding the openness and lightness
of his stadium, with its wholly glazed façade,
Schweizer was a cautious modernist who
warned against 'modernist formalism'. He
chose reinforced concrete because of its
flexibility and its plastic qualities; an all-steel
stadium would, he felt, create too restless
an effect and would be too 'incorporeal' in
the Prater Park setting. He regarded steel
as an irrational element that needed to be
subordinated to the plastic character of architecture; if it were to be used on its own, the
resulting structural form would be completely
swallowed up by the sky and the light.[53]

The ground plan of the Vienna stadium
is a pure ellipse. At every decisive point in
the design process Schweizer gave priority
to sensory interaction with the surrounding
park landscape. Immediately outside the
stadium are trees which project far above the
modest, 14-metre-high stands. The glass in

the recurring façade sections
reflects the shifting foliage,
just as the stadium itself is
reflected in the water of the adjacent
Spiegelteich ('mirror pool'). All ancillary
functions are fitted into the spaces under the
stands thereby removing the need for annexes
between the stadium and the park. The building creates the impression of an archetypical,
almost childishly primitive architecture: stands
consist of little more than a lazy piling up
of steps; entrance corridors lead straight
through to the playing field. The imprints of
the wooden shuttering that are everywhere
in evidence appear to contain a subtle reference to architectural prehistory; they simu-
late an archeology of tree trunks and wood
cabins as a tectonic basis for architecture.

The Vienna stadium is pre-eminently
an open-air stadium. The spatial structure
of the arena appears to be focused upwards
and outwards rather than inwards, while the
pastoral embedding in nature marks the
stadium out as a typical prewar design – a
type that would rapidly lose its appeal after
the 1930s.

The stadium had been commissioned by the
Vienna city council in 1928 with a view to
staging the second international workers'
olympiad there three years later.[54] So it
was that in 1931 Schweizer's functional
facility was the setting for a massive socialist
Festspiel to mark the opening and inauguration of the workers' tournament. The
pageant, written by Robert Ehrenzweig, was
once again about the emancipation of the
proletariat which was presented in unmis-
takable symbolic tableaux.[55] The Arbeiter-
Turn und Sport Zeitung published a particularly lyrical review. 'The crowd portrays itself.
Magnificent and earth-shattering theatre.
5000 participants on the stage which is the
green lawn in the depths of the stadium.
Nor are they alone, the 60,000 spectators
collaborate in equal part.' The greatest
impact was made by the finale in which the
revolutionary awakening of the crowd reached
an ecstatic climax; simultaneously, the final
distinction between actors and audience
was removed by skilful choreography.
'Amidst tumultuous applause, the golden
idol [= capital] sinks and the lights of freedom
swing from the stands, first individual torches
in the joyous chorus, then strings and rivers
of light that circle and fill the huge arena
and billow out through the Marathon Tower
to the singing of the Internationale by
65,000 voices. The public follows the torch-

light procession, which wends its way through the Prater to the town hall. With its great antitheses and slogans elevated to symbols, this spectacle overwhelms crowd and space. The crowd is all movement and colour.'[56]

From this description it is clear that the contrast between a functionalist and a cultic approach to mass accommodation in the 1930 was by no means absolute. In practice there may not even have been any sign of contrast. The Massenspiele, Festspiele and Thingspiele could never have been staged without the logistical ingenuity of a sophisticated stadium design that allowed for quick scene changes and mass movement. Closed formations would have disintegrated without an adequate entrance and exit capacity; the discipline of 'the movement' would have been undermined.

In fact, Schweizer's open stadium of rough concrete, designed for the purpose of 'grasping the needs of the masses',[57] was an ideal space for the development of the crowd as a political body. And the fact that the same architect's Nuremberg sports stadium was one of the locations where, three years later, Leni Riefenstahl shot her film Triumph des Willens (Triumph of the Will; an idealized record of the 1934 Nazi Party convention[58]) lends support to the thesis that the different mass movements were in that respect to some extent interchangeable.[59]

Olympia, Pergamum, Berlin

On 31 October 1934, Adolf Hitler toured the building site of the Olympic Stadium in Berlin. The Chancellor had let it be known beforehand that he wanted to see a full-scale mock-up of a section of the stadium façade. What he saw caused him to fly into a rage: the pillars in the outer gallery were much too thin, and why were they made of concrete instead of stone? On 17 December, the stadium architect, Werner March, presented a modified design in which the pillars had been enlarged from [62] by 85 centimetres to 72 by 100 centimetres. But the ministerial building authority was not satisfied: it was still not 'massive' enough. Moreover, March continued to resist the idea of facing the stadium building with slabs of stone. In February 1935 he was relieved of final responsibility. Albert Speer was brought in and rapidly designed the required aesthetic amendments: the exterior of the concrete stadium was faced with a thick layer of blue stone and instead of a light steel fence, a monumental corbelled cornice appeared on the upper edge of the stand.[60]

Façade of the Vienna Stadium, 1928-1931

The design history of the Reich Sports Field in Berlin, the sports complex for the 1936 Olympic Games, was scarred by this long-drawn-out conflict between the architect and his clients. The principle bone of contention can be summed up in a single word: mass, both qualitative (massiveness, weight) and quantitative (capacity). In the last instance though it was also about the historic mass of the National Socialist regime which had turned the staging of the Games into a matter of political prestige.

After Hitler's election victory in 1933, the international sports world feared that the 1936 Games, which had been awarded to Berlin back in 1931, would be cancelled by the new regime. The National Socialists were known to dislike modern competitive sport which they regarded as inferior to their own national gymnastics tradition.[61] The international sporting movement was seen as a cloak for a Jewish-pacifist plot to weaken German manhood and substitute surrogate competitions for heroic warfare.[62] The fact that the Nazis did not cancel the Berlin Games but positively welcomed them and elevated them to a state occasion, simply meant that they saw in them an opportunity to show off the organizational talent and physical superiority of the German people.[63] Hitler and his Propaganda Minister Goebbels perfectly understood the publicity value of

the Games, with Hitler receiving the representatives of the entire civilized world in his own country.[64]

The building programme for the Olympic complex was drawn up by the Ministry of the Interior. Initially it called for a three-in-one combination of the largest stadium, the largest parade ground and the largest open-air theatre in the world. After the Games were over, this gigantic Festplatz (celebration site) could continue to be used for mass political gatherings. Hitler had stipulated a total capacity of 500,000. His conflict with Werner March began in the very first design phase (October 1933) when the architect suggested expanding the capacity of the existing Grünewald stadium to 100,000, an option already explicitly rejected by Hitler. Invoking his experience with stadia abroad and scientific research into human vision, March insisted that a stadium for half a million people was impracticable. It was therefore decided to separate the three functions (sports arena, parade ground and open-air theatre) and so make it possible to bring together 100,000, 500,000 and 100,000 people respectively at the same time.[65]

Time and again, however, the architect disappointed his clients: the capacity of the open-air theatre he designed was only 35,000 (further reduced to 20,000 in the construction phase). The parade ground

(Aufmarschgelände or Maifeld), including grandstands, could accommodate no more than 200,000.[66] That propaganda played a large role in this conflict became evident in January 1934 when recalculations showed that the combined capacity of the three facilities – 380,000 – was too small for the largest mass gatherings: in press communiqués of the time this shortfall was glossed over by rounding the figure up to 'half a million'.[67]

Like Schweizer's stadium in Vienna (which was an important model for March), the Olympic Stadium in Berlin is proof that there was never an unbridgeable gap between cultic and functionalist approaches to mass accommodation. Under a thin layer of Speer cosmetics is a functional, reinforced concrete skeleton with an efficient access system. The double gallery – an inner gallery 85 centimetre below ground level and an outer gallery one level higher – was a substantial improvement on Schweizer's design. By creating a sunken playing field (-12 metres), March was able to convey the public to the inner gallery between the bottom and top stand levels without stairs. Since the public facilities were located along this gallery, this solution eliminated the worst potential bottleneck in the circulation.[68]

For March, as for Schweizer, it was very important that the structure should blend in with its surroundings. He praised the delicate Brandenburg landscape, even remarking that it reminded him of Japan.[69] By placing a large part of the stadium volume below ground level he was able to avoid dominating the surroundings with a massive lump of masonry without having to sacrifice any of the 100,000 capacity (65,000 seats). The role played by the outer gallery was not only logistical but above all scenic: it offered the public a sweeping view over the surrounding sports park and park landscape. Conversely, the slender concrete columns of the gallery, 'in an ever-changing play of light and shadow', would have the optical effect reducing the massiveness of the structure.[70] This effect was only one of several moments in an extensive visual scenario based on the natural features of the location and the surrounding landscape. The existing park layout, including the hills and dales, was retained as far as possible and integrated into a carefully planned configuration of entrance and exit routes, open spaces and playing fields, static and dynamic points – all geared to the gradual build-up of tension and expectation among the public.[71]

Internal gallery in the Berlin Olympic Stadium, 1936

Even the monumental axial arrangement linking the main stadium, the aquatic stadium, the forecourts, the Maifeld, the other sports fields, the open-air theatre and the feeder roads, played its part in this by dramatizing the succession of elegiac glimpses of scenery at crucial moments.

This dramatic structure merged smoothly with the totalitarian mise-en-scène of the cult of leadership. The longitudinal axis through the elliptically shaped stadium culminated on the other side of the Maifeld in the Stand des Führers (Führer's dais) signalled by a clock tower and a row of flag masts in the centre of a crescent-shaped rostrum beneath which lay the Langemarckhalle, a monument in memory of the German soldiers killed in the First World War battle of Langemarck.[72] The opening in the west wall of the stadium (the marathon gate) meant that the public inside the stadium was in constant spiritual touch with the cultic foundations of the Third Reich. The view thus afforded of the immense Maifeld (290 by 275 metres)

and beyond it Hitler's dais confronted the crowd with the compelling appeal of mass politics. This appeal acquired even more concrete shape in the gymnastic displays on the Maifeld: thousands of young people lined up in long rows, engaged in uniform rhythmic exercises. So although the Nazis did not interfere in the organization of the Games, the politicization of mass sport was a constant background presence.

Such observations do not detract from the highly successful integration of the sports complex with the infrastructure of the city. A vast traffic network was constructed around the stadium geared to the huge numbers of visitors expected. The network structure included a great deal: wide streets linked to the city's main feeder roads; car parks, tram and train stations; bus lanes and dedicated footpaths between the stadium and the railway stations. (Measures aimed at ensuring the efficient movement of one million people, such as extra wide boulevards and the division of the city into seven

Aufmarschbezirke (assembly areas), were rendered superfluous by the revised capacity calculations of January 1934.[73]) At the same time the sports complex was distinguished by its incorporation of the most modern means of communication for both security and journalistic purposes. The Berlin Games were the world's first large-scale television event; distributed around the city were 27 Fernsehstuben (television parlours) where people could follow the proceedings.[74]

While the age of television was just beginning, another cultural era was ending. The Olympic complex in Berlin was simultaneously the climax and the final act of the quest with which modern stadium construction had begun fifty years earlier. Yet not only did it achieve the most balanced integration of the classic amphitheatre with the nineteenth-century sports park, it also formed the culmination of a sporting culture peculiar to the interwar years. A host of tried and tested elements were brought together here in a hyper-intensified form: a concrete skeleton that broke open the mass; an elliptical plan with galleries and decentralized access routes; monumental towers; combined accommodation for sport, theatre and political rallies;[75] and embedment in an idealized nature.[76] Even the linking of the sports complex with a monument to fallen soldiers was neither new nor 'typically Nazi'.[77]

The Nazi contribution to the 1936 Games – the use of pseudo-classical images and theatrical scenic elements designed to make up for the spiritual and emotional shortcomings of competitive sport – did not represent a break with the philosophy of the Olympic movement but rather a logical support and reinforcement of that philosophy. Leni Riefenstahl's two-part film of the Berlin Games, Olympia: Festival of the Nations, Festival of Beauty focused more on the coordinated beauty of athletic bodies in action than on the competitive aspect. In so doing, she was affirming not only the Blut-und-Boden (Blood and Soil) tradition of gymnastics but also De Coubertin's principle that participation was more important than winning. Just as fascism had formalized political ideology into the choreography of a 'movement', devoid of any explicit programme, so the Olympic movement revolved around a form of sacrality devoid of religious content – a transnational cult or religion without ecclesiastical connections.[78] Nor did the use of ritual attributes (flags, olive branches, fire) in the Olympic ceremonial differ much from

'Reichssportfeld' in Berlin, 1936

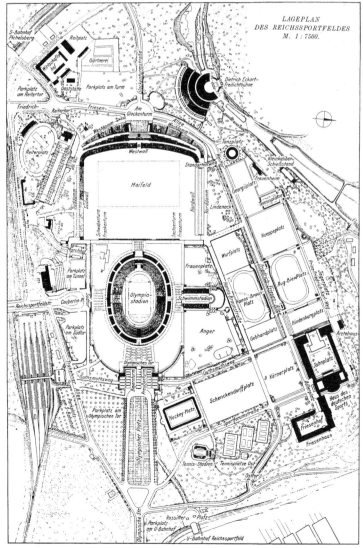

that of other (mass) movements of the interwar period.
The Olympic salute with out-
stretched arm even bore an uncanny resem-
blance to the Nazi salute.[79] In fact both
'Germania' and 'Olympia' amounted to an
artificial reanimation of an imaginary past.
In the opening scenes of Riefenstahl's film
the journey of the torch-bearer from the
shrine at Olympia to the stadium in Berlin is
implicitly used to reconstruct the Third Reich's
roots in the civilization of classic antiquity.
This brief trek through world history was
repeated in Berlin itself: the opening ceremony of the Games began with a solemn
gathering of the International Olympic
Committee at the Pergamum altar in the
Altes Museum from whence the members
processed to the stadium.[80]

On 1 August 1936, the Games opened in
the stadium with a dedicatory Pageant of
Youth involving the choreographer Mary
Wigman, the composers Carl Orff and Werner
Egk, 140 dancers and thousands of flag-
waving, dancing and singing girls and boys.
The spectacle included an ode to the
Olympic flame ('Sacred breath / of purity, /
of beauty, / of fiery spirit / sublime symbol
[...]') and a balletic duel to the death between two 'warriors', ending with a funeral
lament ('The sacred meaning / of all play: /
the highest benefit / to the Fatherland. /
The Fatherland's highest commandment / in
time of crisis: / to sacrifice one's life!').[81]
One day later the adjacent open-air theatre
was the setting for the première of Das
Frankenburger Würfelspiel, the show-piece of
the Thingspiel movement written by Eberhard
Wolfgang Möller. The plot was based on an
incident supposed to have occurred in
1625 during the Thirty Years War, when
several Austrian peasants were forced to
play a game of dice to decide which of
them should be hanged.[82] Just as in the
Olympic inaugural pageant of the previous
day, this allegorical mass spectacle availed
itself of grand gestures, choirs and dramatic
choreographies. The parallel between the
innocent Austrian peasants of 1625 and
the German people under Hitler was expressed in all manner of subtle and not-so-
subtle ways: 'Oh dear God, what do you
want of us? / Nowhere in the whole wide
German empire / are there better Germans
than in Austria'. The suggestion was that
after the drama of 1625, the heroic
national spirit had lodged in a pan-
Germanic collective subconscious, where it

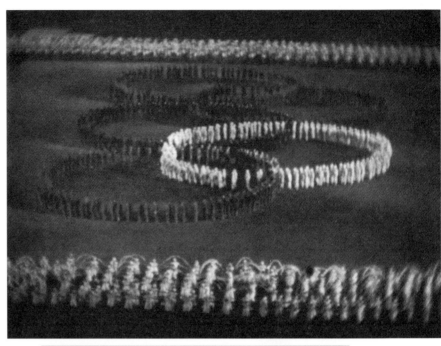

Opening ceremony, Berlin Olympics, 1936
'Das Frankenburger Würfelspiel' in the open air theatre, Berlin Olympics, 1936

had lain dormant until jolted into life by the
arrival of Hitler.[83]

The conjunction of the Olympic
Pageant of Youth and the Germanic spectacle
Das Frankenburger Würfelspiel marks the
historic climax of the interpenetration of
the Olympic and National Socialist move-

ments. It is no accident that after 1945 the
Olympic pageant was abolished along with
the Olympic salute. Those elements of the
Olympic ceremony that have survived to the
present day, like the torch and the flame,
are the fossilized remains of the cultic mass
movements of the interwar years and as

such a final, faded reminder of the stadium as political mass theatre.

Triumph of the ironic crowd

In retrospect, the far-reaching and highly detailed standardization of all kinds of sporting facilities since the Second World War, based on a few ideal types that had taken shape in the 1930s, can be seen as part of a strategy to pacify the masses; a strategy to suspend the antagonism between crowd and architecture by means of sophisticated management techniques and logistical formulas. Le Corbusier's appropriation of the grain silo was stripped of its metaphorical baggage and instrumentalized. Guidelines for the design of mass facilities, such as those in Rudolf Ortner's 1953 handbook Sportbauten (sporting facilities), rely heavily on the rationale of bulk technology. Ortner writes of the importance of 'a frictionless passage to the spectator positions' and 'an unimpeded emptying', as if he is thinking of grains of wheat pouring into or out of a silo.[84] Although Ortner puts the emphasis on design types that have proved themselves in practice (with references to stadia in Florence, Vienna, Turin, Berlin, Rotterdam, Los Angeles and elsewhere) his incorporation of that know-how aspires above all to be value-free and scientific. He adopted the rule of thumb that the evacuation of a sporting facility should take no more than five to ten minutes and used this as his starting point in calculating corridor widths, flow rates and the number of entrances.[85] Optimum standards for the height and shape of grandstands, their gradient, sight lines to the pitch, the positioning of the loudspeaker system, the provision of sanitary facilities and many other matters were all dealt with by Ortner, whose handbook even offered general guidelines as to the number of sporting facilities per municipality, expressed in terms of square metres per inhabitant.

The rise in population and prosperity in post-war Europe, the development of a social-democratic welfare state and the flowering of a new mass culture, were major factors in the rapid growth of the sporting public. With the odd exception, this led not to still larger stadia but to a greater number and wider distribution. In most countries, sporting complexes came to be regarded as a basic municipal amenity. In a situation in which numerous new sporting facilities needed to be built and old ones modernized, the importance of a technical

Stadium washrooms, handbook by Rudolf Ortner, 1953

handbook like Ortner's speaks for itself. In line with the strict functional differentiation of post-war cities (with separate zones for housing, factories, offices, shops and so on) there came an end to the integration of sport, open-air theatre and mass political gatherings in multifunctional facilities. After 1945 there was no longer any ideological basis for such a melding of functions. The emphasis on planning and rationality in post-war reconstruction led to functional differentiation in sporting facilities as well. Accordingly, Ortner's book contained highly detailed standard designs of individual facilities for dozens of different field, track, indoor and aquatic sports.

The next wave of multifunctionality did not begin until the 1980s when stadium attendance, partly as a result of the rise of television sport and negative publicity about supporter behaviour, had reached an all-time low.[86] It was at this point that the commercial exploitation of stadia started to become an end in itself. Mega-pop concerts

were one way of boosting attendance figures. Attendance at sporting events in stadia was made more attractive, even as a family outing, by providing better amenities, replacing terracing with proper seating, and building roofs that reduced exposure to the elements. Instead, there was increased exposure to consumption and entertainment. The crowd was coddled and cosseted; spectators turned into consumers.

In the spirit of Canetti one may wonder whether all these efforts to pacify the crowd are really capable of lasting success. The long list of crushes and stampedes of the past hundred years suggests not. The metaphor of the human avalanche[87] is the most expressive but not the only indication that the bulk materials theory employed in modern stadium architecture (as in the rule that stands should always be 'filled' from the top downwards[88]) makes dangerous use of the inherent dynamism of the crowd. The bloody incidents with their unpredictable causes demonstrate how easily bulk technology can end in uncontrollable effects

Stamford Bridge Stadium in Liverpool, 1945

that turn against both crowd and architecture: whichever 'skeleton' is the weaker – human bones or stone walls – will be the first to give way.

Yet it is difficult to deny that the strategy of pacification has been relatively successful. If it were possible to watch a speeded up video tape of the history of modern stadium construction what one would see is one long-drawn-out and continuous encapsulation of the crowd. This movement, as of a slowly closing oyster, is reiterated symbolically by the sliding roofs with which the latest batch of stadia from the 1990s have been fitted. While Schweizer's stadium in Vienna had terraces for 50,000, was completely open to the skies and had a strong relationship with the surrounding landscape, the Amsterdam ArenA (1992-1996) is a fully enclosed, all-seater stadium that effectively erases the final distinction between a sports stadium and an events hall. As such the development from a standing to a seated audience and from open to closed facilities appears to be complete.

During the past twenty years the financial structure of professional sport has come increasingly to be dominated by television rights, the value of which has risen explosively. The global television audience has turned sport into an exceptionally lucrative market for sponsors and advertisers. Without this escalating flow of money, the new multi-purpose facilities of the 1990s might never even have been built. This helps to explain why such stadia, like the Amsterdam ArenA and the Stade de France in Paris (1998), should have acquired the character of a shuttered, blank-walled box that is totally impervious to its urban or spatial context. In reality they are little more than overgrown television studios.

The public experience of major sporting events no longer takes place in the stadium but in front of the television screen. Given the global coverage of the multi-stage system of television rights, the presence of spectators in the stadium is futile and superfluous, at least in terms of numbers. But the format of the sports broadcast requires that, just as for quiz, entertainment and chat shows, there should still be a relatively small token audience present in the 'studio' during recordings, an audience whose task it is to create a telegenic ambience into which the viewers at home can project themselves.

Seen from the perspective of the living room, the hermetic and decontextualized character of contemporary stadia suddenly becomes perfectly comprehensible. As television studios it matters not one jot where they are located. On television, all stadia are placeless and identical. The architect Michel Lévi has described this disconnection in an essay on the Stade de France. '[The stadium] is subordinated to the tv media and the potential enormous financial profit. It is just because 80,000 people communicate together at a game that 3.7 billion tv spectators may communicate with them or rather have that impression, as if they were there, through the illusion of a total fusion. Thus the stadium is organized for this possible ritual identification. It is a self-contained totality, closed around itself and its symbolism. The physical context in which the stadium is set does not belong to this media-related system and is taken into account only insofar as controlling it may help the stadium to function well. In other words, the context is not a dynamic element of the architectural design, and the stadium logically looks like an isolated object, disconnected from its setting; it is an object which could have been built anywhere.'[89]

The official inquiry into the Hillsborough stadium disaster in 1989 resulted in the inquiry judge recommending that all terraces in football stadia be replaced by seating. This recommendation was adopted by the British government and made a statutory requirement in 1990. The UEFA followed suit shortly thereafter: starting with the 1994-95 season, terraces were banned for all European matches.[90] The safety argument was an unintended godsend for club managers who had been trying since the late 1980s to bring football culture into line with the dominant free-market ideology. The new safety requirements not only represented a golden opportunity for redevelopment and investment; given the smaller capacity and greater comfort of all-seater stands, they also provided an argument for raising ticket prices and thus an instrument for upgrading the social composition of the stadium public.[91] It was thus no accident that the measures by which the clubs managed to achieve a new, economic relationship with their clients in the 1990s proved to have far-reaching consequences for the traditional supporter culture of the terraces. This break was most keenly felt in England where class consciousness has always been more intense and the football stadia were more run down than elsewhere in Europe. In the Netherlands a comparable cultural revolution was sparked off by Ajax football club's move to the new Amsterdam ArenA.

The traditional, masculine supporter culture has been described as an 'invented tradition' that in reality dates back no further than the 1960s and the emergence of a relatively well-off working-class public.[92] In this subculture, the physical experience of standing pressed together on the terraces was the pivot around which the emotional experience of football revolved. The club served as a medium for masculine solidarity among a hard core of supporters; the love felt for one's own club was tantamount to love of the sense of belonging generated by the collective experience in the crowd. 'The love for the team is a transposed love of the lads' own social groups and the masculinity which informs that group's relations with itself and others. The team, and the love invested in it, is a symbol of the values and friendships which exist between the lads. The love which the lads invest in the team affirms their notion of themselves as lads and their relations to each other at the deepest and most effective level.'[93] During the weekly ritual in the stadium certain emotional barriers fell away, as the following admission by a 27 year-old Manchester City fan reveals: 'I reckon it's surrogate emotions, I really do. I think it's all these blokes that just can't say "I love you." I can't say, "oh, you're a really good bloke, you are" but I can sing at the top of my voice, "I love you City" or "We love you City," or I can cry when we get promoted or I can cry when we get relegated . But if my mum dropped dead I probably wouldn't cry ....'[94]

The old terraces formed an enclosed space in which emotional solidarity could reach ecstatic heights. Now that this terracing has largely disappeared, group formation has become more difficult. Seeking one another out, singing, waving and chanting in unison does not occur so spontaneously when everyone is sitting in individual bucket seats. The fans feel as if they have landed up in a cinema. 'When it was all paddocks, it was all crushed in and everyone was swaying about and jumping about, and waving their fist at the opposition over the fence and all that. Now, it's not the same at all, it's almost like going to the cinema ....'[95] In contemporary all-seater stadium design, the fear of touch described by Canetti has in effect been sublimated, with the result that crowd formation is blocked.

The reaction of supporters to the attack on their subculture in the 1990s was a mixture of resignation and resistance. At Manchester United – the club that more than any other in Europe has transformed itself into a purely commercial enterprise – the regular supporters attempted to keep up the collective rituals by all standing up during a match and remaining standing for long periods to the accompaniment of the song Stand Up for the Champions. The club management did everything it could to quash this practice, including posters in the stadium and warnings over the loudspeaker system.[96] Exactly the same confrontation occurred in section 127 of the Amsterdam ArenA: Stand Up If You Love Ajax. According to an article in the fanzine De Ajax Ster, overbearing stewards ordered supporters to remain seated and the club chairman threatened to have persistent offenders banned from entering the stadium.[97] In both Manchester and Amsterdam the club management appealed to safety arguments.

Another possible explanation for the club managers' campaign to suppress the masculine subculture of the old terraces in the 1990s is the sense of menace and reined-in energy radiated by a standing crowd. 'A standing man creates an impression of energy which is as yet unused. ... A standing man may do anything, and our respect for him derives partly from the fact that so many possibilities are open to him, that he is alert and able to move at any moment. But we expect someone who is sitting to remain sitting. ... The simplest form of power is that derived from a man's own body and he can express it either in terms of height – in which case he must stand – or in terms of weight – in which case he must exert visible pressure. To stand up from a sitting position is to do both.'[98]

What is left of the old terrace culture has been effectively hijacked (suitably sanitized, of course) in the interests of atmosphere creation. In the Amsterdam ArenA the sound of hard core fans is broadcast in amplified form to the VIP stand. Whenever a racist slur is aired, the volume down is turned down.

At the beginning of the twenty-first century one cannot but conclude that television was the instrument that made possible the complete pacification of the crowd. The crowd

Manchester United poster in Old Trafford Stadium

STANDING - AN URGENT PROBLEM

UNLESS SUPPORTERS REMAIN SEATED THROUGHOUT THE MATCH - OTHER THAN MOMENTARILY AT TIMES OF GREAT EXCITEMENT, THERE IS A REAL POSSIBILITY THAT THE CAPACITY OF THIS SECTION MAY BE SUBSTANTIALLY REDUCED.

YOUR CO-OPERATION WOULD BE VERY MUCH APPRECIATED BY EVERYONE AT MANCHESTER UNITED.

has been scattered, dispersed, domesticated – in short, sent home. Those left behind in the stadium stand for the invisible collective of the viewers at home. Like the sponsors, they address themselves directly to the television cameras by holding up banners with witty texts aimed at the home front. As such, the 1990s were characterized by a new type of fan, a fan who has grown up with sport on television. Well educated and well paid, he or she comes to the stadium to play their part in a consciously contrived 'crowd'. So it was that the century of mass sport culminated in the triumph of the ironic crowd. The subculture of the football fan has been partially adopted by more affluent social strata; some of the new fans imagine themselves members of an authentic working class, even going so far as to acquire the corresponding accent.[99] In progressive and intellectual circles supporter status has ceased to be an embarrassment. The ironic crowd has its own ironic fanzines: semi-literary magazines like When Saturday Comes (English) and Hard Gras (Dutch), in which the reconstruction of an idyllic football past is charged with melancholic reflections about its disappearance.[100]

In the long run, the primitive power struggle between the hard core of supporters who want to remain standing and the club management who wants everybody to be seated will probably be quietly smothered in the ironic television variant of mass insurrection: the 'wave', the telegenic symbol par excellence of the ironic crowd.

Stade de France in Paris, 1998

1. Elias Canetti, Crowds and Power [1960], transl. Carol Stewart 1962, (London: Penguin Books, 1973), p.31.
2. H.A. van Wijnen, De Kuip. De geschedenis van het stadion Feyenoord (Utrecht/Antwerp: Veen, 1989), p. 69; N. Luning Prak, 'De bouw van het stadion feyenoord', in: Bulletin van de Koninklijke Nederlandse Oudheidkundige Bond, vol. 69, 1970, p. 144.
3. Desmond Morris, The Soccer Tribe (London: Jonathan Cape, 1981), pp.272-73); Simon Inglis, The Football Grounds of Great Britain (London: Willow Books, 1987), pp. 28-29.
4. Quotations taken from: Rogan Taylor, Andrew Ward, Tim Newburn (eds), The Day of the Hillsborough Disaster. A Narrative Account (Liverpool: Liverpool University Press, 1995), pp. 49, 52, 58.
5. Canetti, Crowds and Power, p.29.
6. Ibid., p. 15.
7. Ibid., pp. 15-16.
8. Morris, The Soccer Tribe, pp. 272-78; Inglis, The Football Grounds of Great Britain, pp. 28-39; Leon Mann, 'Sports Crowds Viewed from the Perspective of Collective Behavior', in: Jeffrey H. Goldstein (ed.), Sports, games, and Play. Social and Psychological Viewpoints (Hillsdale, N.J.: Lawrence Erlbaum Ass. Publishers, 1979), p. 348 ff.
9. Canetti, Crowds and Power, p. 21.
10. Ibid., p. 21.
11. Ibid., p. 17.
12. Ibid., pp. 18, 33.
13. Ibid., p. 38.
14. Ibid., pp. 38.
15. Ibid., p. 23.
16. Ibid., pp. 99.
17. Moshé, Zwarts, quoted in: Tijs Tummers, Architectuur aan de zijlijn. Stadions en tribunes in Nederland (Amsterdam: D'ARTS, 1993), p. 80.
18. John M. Hoberman, Sport and Political Ideology (London: Heinemann, 1984), p. 123.
19. Ibid., pp. 39-45. See also: J. Huizinga, Homo Ludens: A Study of the Play Element in Culture (London: Paladin, 1970) and J. Ortega y Gasset, ' The Sportive Origin of the State' (1924), in: idem, History as a System (New York: Norton, 1961).
20. Hoberman, Sport and Political Ideology, pp. 124-25.

21. Ibid., p. 146. See also: Robert Musil, 'Als Papa Tennis lernte' [1931], in: idem, Tagebücher, Aphorismen, Essays und Reden, ed. Adolf Frisé, (Hamburg: Rowohlt, 1955), pp. 815-20.
22. Hoberman, Sport and Political Ideology, pp. 160-61.
23. Henning Eichberg, 'Thing-, Fest- und Weihespiele in Nationalsozialismus, Arbeiterkultur und Olympismus. Zur Geschichte des politischen Verhaltens in der Epoche des Faschismus', in: Eichberg et al., Massenspiele. NS-Thingspiel, Arbeiterweihespiel und olympisches Zeremoniell (Stuttgart-Bad Cannstatt: Frommann-Holzboog, 1977), pp. 155-56.
24. Johannes Seiffert, Anlagen für Sport und Spiel (Leipzig: J.M. Gebhardt's Verlag, 1928), pp. 139-44. See also: Franz-Joachim Verspohl, Stadionbauten von der Antike bis zur Gegenwart. Regie und Selbsterfahrung der Massen (Gießen: Anabas-Verlag, 1976), pp. 187-90.
25. Seiffert, Anlagen für Sport und Spiel, pp. 145-52.
26. Cf. Eichberg, 'Thing-, Fest- und Weihespiele'. The Thingspiel movement took its cue from the ancient Teutonic custom of the public assembly or 'Thing'.
27. Quoted in: ibid., p. 69.
28. Ibid., p. 67.
29. Ibid., pp. 74-75.
30. Quoted in: ibid., p. 77.
31. Ibid., pp. 86-89.
32. Ibid., pp.79-105.
33. Ibid., p. 160.
34. Ibid., pp. 113, 119-20.
35. Ibid., pp. 123-29. See also Martin Loiperdinger, Der Parteitagsfilm 'Triumph des Willens' von Leni Reifenstahl. Rituale der Mobilmachung (Opladen: Leske & Budrich, 1987), p. 139.
36. Eichberg, 'Thing-, Fest- und Weihespiele', pp. 54-64.
37. Ibid., p. 61.
38. Ibid., pp. 56-58.
39. Quoted in: ibid., p. 56.
40. Ibid., p. 183.
41. Verspohl, Stadionbauten, p. 162 ff.
42. Ibid., p. 163; and Barclay F. Gordon, Olympic Architecture. Building for the Summer Games (New York: John Wiley, 1983), pp. 6-7.

43. Verspohl, Stadionbauten, pp. 193-97.
44. Immo Boyken, Otto Ernst Schweizer 1890-1965. Bauten und Projekte (Stuttgart: Edition Axel Menges, 1996), pp. 102-13.
45. Gordon, Olympic Architecture, p. 9.
46. Verspohl, Stadionbauten, pp.165-66.
47. Gordon, Olympic Architecture, p. 18.
48. Tummers, Architectuur aan de zijlijn, p. 51.
49. Gordon, Olympic Architecture, p. 12.
50. Canetti, Crowds and Power, p. 23.
51. Boyken, Otto Ernst Schweizer, p. 120.
52. Luning Prak, 'De bouw van het stadion Feyenoord', p. 142.
53. Boyken, Otto Ernst Schweizer, pp. 24-25.
54. Ibid., p. 120.
55. Eichberg, 'Thing-, Fest- und Weihespiele', p. 90.
56. Quotes taken from: ibid., pp. 90-91.
57. Schweizer, quoted in: Boyken, Otto Ernst Schweizer, p. 21.
58. Loiperdinger, Der Parteitagsfilm, pp. 64-65.
59. Eichberg, 'Thing-, Fest- und Weihespiele', pp. 155-56.
60. Thomas Schmidt, Werner March. Architekt des Olympia-Stadions 1894-1976 (Basle: Birkhäuser Verlag, 1992), pp. 46-48. In his 1969 memoirs, Speer claimed to have also scrapped the 'glazed intermediate surfaces' of the building, but this element had already vanished (if it had indeed ever existed) from March's own construction drawings of August 1934. See Albert Speer, Inside the Third Reich (New York: MacMillan, 1970), p. 95.
61. Allen Guttmann, The Games Must Go On. Avery Brundage and the Olympic Movement (New York: Columbia University Press, 1984), pp. 62-63.
62. Hoberman, Sport and Political Ideology, p. 166.
63. Guttmann, The Games Must Go On, p. 65.
64. Verspohl, Stadionbauten, pp. 240-42.
65. Schmidt, Werner March, pp. 30-32.
66. Ibid., p. 32.
67. Ibid., p. 39.
68. Cf. Werner March, Bauwerk Reichssportfeld (Berlin: Deutscher Kunstverlag, 1936), p. 22.
69. Schmidt, Werner March, p. 36.
70. March, Bauwerk Reichssportfeld, p. 24.
71. Ibid., pp. 16-17.
72. Ibid., pp. 28-29.
73. Schmidt, Werner March, p. 40.
74. Allen Guttmann, Sports Spectators (New York: Columbia University Press, 1986), p. 134.
75. Compare the sports park in Frankfurt am Main.
76. Verspohl, Sportbauen, p. 247.
77. Compare the Los Angeles Memorial Coliseum (1922-32) and the Soldiers Field Stadium in Chicago (c. 1920).
78. Eichberg, 'Thing-, Fest- und Weihespiele', pp. 146-47.
79. Ibid., pp. 147-49.
80. March, Bauwerk Reichssportfeld, p. 16.
81. Eichberg, 'Thing-, Fest- und Weihespiele', pp. 143-45. (The libretto was written by Carl Diem, in charge of organizing the Games.) [head of the Games organization.)]
82. Glen W. Gladberry, 'Eberhard Wolfgang Möller's Thingspiel Das Frankenburger Würfelspiel', in: Eichberg et al., Massenspiele. NS-Thingspiel, Arbeiterweihespiel und olympisches Zeremoniell (Stuttgart-Bad Cannstatt: Frommann-Holzboog, 1977), pp. 238-39.
83. Ibid., pp. 242-43.
84. Rudolf Ortner, Sportbauten. Anlage, Bau, Ausstattung (Munich: Verlag Georg D.W. Callwey, 1953), p. 29.
85. Ibid., p. 30.
86. Between the 1948-49 and 1985-86 seasons, total attendance figures for English Football League matches dropped from 41.3 to 16.5 million. See: Anthony King, The End of the Terraces. The Transformation of English Football in the 1990s (London/New York: Leicester University Press, 1998), p. 38.
87. Morris, The Soccer Tribe, p. 275.
88. Tummers, Architecture aan de zijlijn, p. 59.
89. Michel Lévi, 'A Monument to Our Futility. The Stade de France in La Plaine Something-Denis', in Archis (1998) 6, p. 11.
90. King, The End of the Terraces, pp. 97-98.
91. Ibid., pp. 88-106, 134-41.
92. Ibid., pp. 164-65.
93. Ibid., p. 152.
94. Quoted in: ibid.
95. Quoted in ibid., p. 161.
96. Ibid., pp. 162-63, 175.
97. 'Stand or sit?', in: De Ajax Ster (1997) 11. Can also be found on: http://www2.euro-net.nl/users/pi_alfa/loep6e.htm
98. Canetti, Crowds and Power, pp. 449-53.
99. King, The End of the Terraces, p. 183.
100. Ibid., pp. 176-92.

Big

Estadio municipal do Maracana

name: Estadio municipal do Maracana
place: Rio de Janeiro, Brazil
date of construction: 1947-1950
architect: unknown
capacity: 140,000

The biggest stadium ever built stands in Rio de Janeiro. With a capacity of 200,000 (currently reduced to 140,000 owing to tougher safety measures and the poor state of building) the Maracana Stadium is the supreme shrine for football-mad Brazil.

The circular stadium has two cantilevered rings of stands. The structure of the second ring, which is completely separate from first, also supports the all-round roof. Sixty trusses are needed to bear the weight of the four-centimetre-thick roof.

At their highest point the stands are only 23 metres high. In order to create the required number of places the stand ascends at a very low gradient which greatly increases the distance from the pitch. The majority of spectators are seated beyond the point at which it is possible to recognize individual players. But in a country where the motions of the samba and the gaiety of carnival have combined to produce the characteristic samba-football, the carnival atmosphere in the stands is every bit as important as the game being played out on the pitch.

Amphi-teatrum Flavium (Colosseum)

name: Amphitheatrum Flavium (Colosseum)
place: Rome, Italy
date of construction: 72-80
architect: unknown
capacity: 50,000

The Colosseum in Rome is the largest and best known building of Roman antiquity and it displays the technical skill of the Romans in combination with their virtuoso formgiving. The building owes its name to the colossal statue of Nero that once stood beside it.

The oval stadium could accommodate 50,000 spectators and had 'boxes' for the emperor and other dignitaries. The gently rising stand consists of three tiers, the top one of which was for the common folk and women, while the lowest was reserved for the highest class. A colonnade all round forms the exterior of the stadium.

The oval arena was used mainly for the popular gladiatorial contests and could be flooded for staging mock sea battles. Below ground level was an extensive network of corridors and rooms where the gladiators and wild animals waited to be sent out into the arena.

The system of arches supporting the marble stands (the uppermost stands were of wood) were well able to cope with the arrival and departure of large groups of people.

Because the Colosseum was used as a stone quarry during the Middle Ages, a large part of the outer wall, the stand floors and the decoration have been lost. Despite this the stadium has retained its power and beauty and is justifiably regarded as the 'mother of all stadia'. It has served as model for countless modern stadia and remains a potent source of inspiration for today's stadium builders.

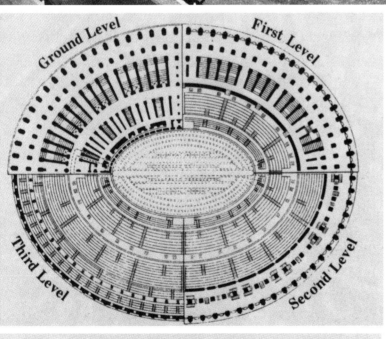

Ground Level

First Level

Third Level

Second Level

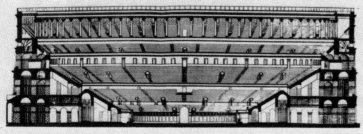

Stadio Guiseppe Meazza (San Siro)

name: Stadio Guiseppe Meazza (San Siro)
place: Milan, Italy
date of construction: 1926
architect: unknown
capacity: 35,000
first major enlargement: 1954
architects: Armando Ronca and Ferruccio Calzolari
capacity: 100,000
second major enlargement: 1990
architects: Ragazzi & Hoffner
capacity: 83,107

The home base of the famous AC Milan and Internazionale football clubs is better known as San Siro, even though it was officially renamed in 1979 after one of Italy's greatest footballers, Guiseppe Meazza.

Extensive renovations for the 1990 World Cup resulted in an all-seater stadium with numbered plastic seats. To compensate the reduced capacity, the stadium was enlarged with a third tier carried by eleven freestanding, cylindrical towers; the four corner towers support the imposing roof structure. This enlargement operation put that of 1954 in the shadow.

In the early 1950s, when the two Milan-based clubs took turns at winning the championship, the ground's capacity was found wanting. Taking the Feyenoord Stadium in the Netherlands as model, a second cantilevered tier was built on top of the existing stands, enabling as many as 100,000 people to attend a match. To provide access to the new area, engineer Calzolari and architect Ronca built nineteen ramps along the façade. The result was a compact stadium with a unique exterior.

Beneath all the alterations it is still possible to recognize the stadium that AC Milan built in 1926: the lowest tier is still largely original. The early stadium consisted of four separate stands, one covered grandstand and three uncovered seater stands. It is not surprising that Milan supporters have difficulty with the present name of their stadium. For although Meazza played for AC Milan for two years, he is inextricably associated with arch rival Inter with whom he played no fewer than fourteen seasons.

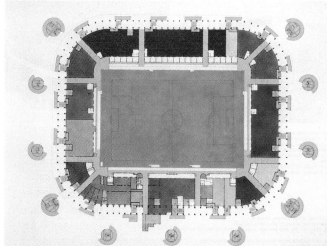

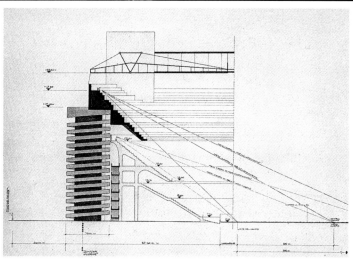

Estadio Santiago Bernabeu Nou Camp

name: Estadio Santiago Bernabeu
place: Madrid, Spain
date of construction: 1944-1947
architects: L. Alemany Soler & M. Muñoz
Monasterio
enlargement: 1954
renovation: 1980
capacity: 90,000

name: Nou Camp
place: Barcelona, Spain
date of construction: 1954-1957
architects: J. Sooteras Mauiri &
F. Mitjans Miró
enlargement: 1980-1982, 1994
enlargement: 1994
capacity: 115,000

Apart from politics (football was especially important under General Franco) and the enormous growth of Real Madrid and F.C. Barcelona football clubs, it was above all the introduction of the European Cup of Champions Cup (between national league champions) in 1955 that led to the construction of larger stadia in Spain (with a similar trend manifesting itself in Italy). The growing number of spectators wanting to attend matches forced the clubs to expand their accommodation. Inspired by Maracana Stadium in Brazil, Barcelona built Nou Camp and Real Madrid built Bernabeu Stadium.

Estadio Santiago Bernabeu was inaugurated in 1947. It was completely open to the skies and consisted of two tiers of stands on three sides and one low terrace on the east side. In 1954 the terrace was replaced by the 'amfitheatro', a three-tier stand wedged between the two corner towers. Right on time for Real Madrid's

dream debut in Europe (the club won five European Cups in a row) the stadium was able to accommodate 120,000 spectators.

The stadium was completely renovated for the 1982 World Cup series. The three low stands were furnished with a lightweight and aerodynamic cantilevered roof made up of two layers. Precisely above the goal areas these layers diverge slightly to make room for the video boards. Where the tall amfitheatro obstructs the roof's circuit the latter is abruptly severed and the two layers are squeezed together in the middle.

Construction of Nou Camp began in 1954. The design was based on Feyenoord Stadium in the Netherlands and like its model had two all-round, cantilevered tiers of seating with a cantilevered roof above the grandstand. But instead of concrete, the architects Soteras Muari and Mitjans Mirõ used steel. The stadium was enlarged and modernized for the 1982 World Cup. A third

tier of seating was added and the exterior and huge scoreboards also date from this time. Real Madrid is inseparably linked to the Spanish establishment, whether it be Franco, the royal house or the Spanish state. These classy connections are reflected in the stadium's location on the city's main avenue, the Castellana, where it occupies a prominent position among the ministries, banks and museums.

'Barca', on the other hand, the standard-bearer of Catalan identity, has founded its own empire. In addition to the football stadium of the same name, Nou Camp, FC Barcelona's new, 15-hectare base boasts an indoor sports hall, a small sports hall, an ice rink, training facilities and a 'Mini-Estadi'. With 110,000 members, Barcelona is the biggest football club in the world but it also plays basketball, roller hockey (after football the leading sport in Spain), handball, volleyball, judo, ice hockey, rugby, athletics and baseball.

CAMP

F.C.B.

NOU

© Licencia F.C. BARCELONA

Centralny Stadion Lenina

name: Centralny Stadion Lenina
place: Moscow, Russia
date of construction: 1956
architect: Polikarpov
capacity: 100,000

A monumental statue of Lenin – proud, jutting chin, overcoat slung loosely over the shoulders and cap in the left hand – marks the entrance to the national stadium named after him. The fact that nearly all Russian stadia bear his name or that of Stalin or some other party bigwig shows the extent to which sport was an integral part of the communist system. Not only was sport wielded as a propaganda tool, but the stadia themselves were used for political rallies and festivities. This stadium, built at a time when mega-stadia were appearing all over the East Bloc, consists entirely of unroofed seats. A regime that propagates equality can scarcely make a distinction between expensive covered seats and cheap terraces in its international calling card.

Russian stadia are nearly always part of huge sports complexes and the park around Lenin Stadium is one of the largest in the world. In addition to the stadium, Luzhiniki Park contains a sports palace for 13,000 spectators, an indoor pool seating 10,500, a sports hall holding 4,000, 22 small sports halls, 11 football pitches, 4 athletic tracks, 3 skating rinks and 55 tennis courts. On top of this, the area beneath the stands houses a cinema, a theatre, a hotel, a restaurant and a medical sports centre. An average of 10,000 people make use of one or more of the 140 different sporting facilities daily.

By Russian standards (the architecture of the time was dominated by decorative Stalinesque baroque) the design of the stadium façade is extremely restrained. It has a classical main frame of columns with cornice beneath which is an open arcade. Above this the architect introduced a vertical articulation in the form of two rows of elongated windows arranged in groups of three. The continuous cornice and the repetition provide a horizontal counterweight. The stadium stands on the bank of the Moscow river and is connected via a central axis with that of the University of Moscow on the other side of the water so that it is part of a monumental spatial composition.

Lenin Stadium (nowadays better known as Luzhiniki) is the home of Spartak Moskow football club and is also used for Russian national team matches. In 1980 the sports park acquired international fame as the setting for the Olympic Games. Two years later the Lenin Stadium hit the news headlines in less fortunate circumstances. On a bitterly cold evening during a UEFA Cup qualifying match against Haarlem Football Club, a group of departing spectators started to slide on an icy ramp. They collided fatally with a crowd of Spartak fans who were trying to re-enter the stadium after hearing that their club had managed to score the winning goal in the final minutes of the game. Estimates of the death toll vary from 69 to 340.

Intervie

HOK-

'Enhance the passio

1

2

After the merger between HOK and LOBB in 1999, HOK+LOBB was the world's largest architectural practice specializing in sports buildings. It has produced some 300 stadia. The practice is currently working on the Olympic Stadium for Games in Sydney in 2000.

How would you describe the changing design of stadia?
Rod Sheard (principal) In the middle of the nineteenth century the English started changing the way sport functioned. Before that, sport was a collection of people in a community, playing another community, and it was really a participation process. Most of the sports that we now know as western sports weren't codified till late or mid-nineteenth century. Rules were applied to them, which allowed you to compare results. Suddenly sport became a spectator exercise, because you could actually compare how your town or your community could do against another. So that really lead to spectators wanting to go to these events. The industrial revolution allowed people to have a little bit of spare time, a little bit of money available to actually visit these events. The railway network across Europe started to spread so it was possible to actually get from one town to another. The British codified rugby, football, soccer, cricket and all of their sports during the nineteenth century. So the first generation of stadia evolved out of that simple require-

ment of allowing people into a field or a stadium bowl and therefore the finances of these buildings were totally structured around how much money you could get people to pay to see your event. These stadia were about allowing people to come in, taking money off them at the gate, letting them sit down, watch an event and then go home again, and that was it.

The first television broadcasts were probably in about 1937. It took about 15 years before the effect could really be felt, particularly in sport. After the Second World War in the fifties you find, certainly in Britain and in a lot of continental countries, the biggest crowds stadia have ever attracted. When you see a photograph of Chelsea and other clubs in those years, they have 100,000 people gathered around, all standing up or sitting on rooftops. About the same time television started to make its influence felt, because that same sporting event was also broadcast on television and people started to stay away. It seemed a lot easier to just sit at home and watch television to see the game. Stadia managers generally said to themselves well, if we want to attract people out of their homes to come to our events then we have to do something more than just give them a place to stand. We have to give them some concourses, places where they can buy food and beverages, and toilets. All of these simple requirements.

w with
LOBB
watching the event'

3   4   5   6

So that second generation of stadia came out of the influence of television and was aimed at putting facilities on the concourses. It very gradually became something more than just sitting watching sport, it started to become a bit more of a social event.

The next big change really happened in 1955. That's when Walt Disney opened Disneyland in California and said: 'All who enter here shall find happiness and knowledge', which was a strange thing for him to say, because happiness was relatively obvious, but knowledge was a bit unusual. He was the first who made clear that the future of leisure was all about providing information in an attractive, interesting and an absorbable way that the general public would enjoy. The other thing he recognised was the importance of entertaining a whole family. The second generation of stadia suffered from the fact that the only people who went to sport, back in the sixties and seventies, were white, male and aged between 18 and 34. You could take almost any sport in the western world and 90% of the audience would fall into that social grouping. Women, children and other people didn't go as they felt uncomfortable. So Walt Disney proved for the first time that you could take a whole family to an event, either a theme park or a sporting event, and entertain them in differ-

1-6. Millennium Stadium in Cardiff, 1999

ent ways for a whole day. The third generation of stadia started as a result of the lead Walt Disney gave to the rest of the leisure industry. It said that sport is very much a part of the leisure industry. That means you have to start providing more than just the odd burger place or hot drinks stand; you have to give the people what Walt provided in the theme parks: video game locations for kids, nice bars and live music etcetera. We are seeing a lot of those third generation stadia today. There is really no limit to what you can pack into it – multiplex cinemas, shopping centres – and that's great because it builds a critical mass and therefore the probability of achieving a level of enjoyment and entertainment.

Right now we are developing what we describe as the fourth generation stadia. The fourth generation started in 1969 which was a pretty amazing year as man walked on the moon for the first time, the Concorde and the jumbo-jet flew for the first time and carried a large amount of people around the world. But the single most amazing thing that happened in 1969 was that three American military computers were linked together and started the Internet. The Internet is changing our lives fairly dramatically, but it is going to change sport out of all recognition of anything we have ever seen before.

The Internet is the conduit for sport into the next century. Digital information distils a game of soccer or cricket into a bunch of zeros and ones. Once that game is distilled it can be extruded down a cable or through a satellite anywhere in the world instantly. That digital information can carry everything from sound to video to all sorts of other statistics about the game. In the future it will even carry a wider range of things like the smell of the game.

So once you can digitize a sporting event then the venue starts to take on a very different form. The first three generations were all about the live audience. The fourth generation for the first time recognises that there are two audiences to every event: the live audience which goes to the trouble of actually going there, and the much larger remote audience, the detached audience. Right now that detached audience relies on Ted Turner or Rupert Murdoch deciding to broadcast that event. In the future you will be able to call up via your computer on your desk anywhere in the world, at any time, any sporting event that is going on. These new fourth generation stadia are all about wiring them up, digitally setting them up. There are a lot of remote digital cameras and sound systems in the pitch and fibre optic backbone runs through the whole building. It is literally a very sophisticated studio. The event that takes place on that piece of grass for those 90 minutes is packaged and sent around the world in so many different formats and so many different ways that the remote audience is gradually growing bigger and bigger.

The size of the live audience is limited. Our Olympic Stadium in Sydney, with 110,000 seats, is probably pushing the limit. A stadium with 80,000 or 90,000 seats has a reasonable balance between contact with the event and distance away. So the live audience is going to be finite, the amount of money people will pay to go to an event is finite, the amount of money that people spend once they are in the stadium is also finite. What is not finite is the sheer number of people who are well away from the stadium and who are prepared to pay for that signal.

Some interesting statistics have come out in the last year or so. There was a round-the-world yacht race called the Whitbread Round the World Race which is held about every four years. A team of about 20 boats sail around the world and fight it out on the southern oceans. No live audience at all, as nobody pays to go and see it. They had 500 million hits on their website during the nine months of the race and suddenly

everybody sat back and said 'Wow! this is a whole new world.' It was a particularly good and clever website, because it was written in such a way that you could put your own boat in the race and choose a course or the sort of sails you set, besides which you could download all the weather and sea information from the Internet. Suddenly it became an interactive Internet link. This development has now been taken to the next step in the BT Global Challenge, the next big round-the-world ocean yacht race which sets off in the year 2000. All the boats have a 24-hour constant uplink through the satellite-network, so at any time anywhere in the world you can patch in to any of the 22 yachts. You are just sitting at your desk, perhaps typing away and you have an on-screen image of what is happening in the southern ocean.

That was the next step. The step after that has just been launched: it is called the virtual spectator. The problem with yacht-racing is again that the Turners and the Murdochs of this world can't broadcast all of the races because it is too difficult and too expensive to get out there in the middle of the ocean. They have modelled exact replicas of the boats taking place in the race in the computer. So what they actually broadcast is a simulated event with computerized boats. You can watch the race from all different angles and have all the statistics about where they are heading, but it is yours to control as you can manage the information you receive. Anybody who has seen A Bug's Life or Toy Story will recognize that the computerization of real life is gaining spectacular strength. What you can most certainly do within ten years is to have a computer model of every football player, rugby

player or cricket player. As the players go out on the field they will be playing in clothes which are electronically tagged, so the computer knows every movement of every player at every time. You will be watching a simulated soccer event, but you won't be able to tell the difference. The amazing thing about this is, that all kinds of statistics will spill out of this kind of computerization. You will be able to know how many times one particular player has run up the field, how many times he has run to the left rather than to the right.

So what it all comes down to is that you won't need stadia at all. All you need is a big tin shed with these players just doing their bit and that signal being distributed around the world in many different ways. But then you would have no atmosphere, no passion and no connection with the event. The technology will develop anyway because there is huge money involved. Nobody is going to stop this process. What we as architects can do is to not let sport drift into a black box, but develop the type of building that allows people to enjoy the event and to enhance the passion to some extent. Sport is all about the passion of watching an event. Future stadia are therefore all about not losing that passion. I think that our job is all about creating an event arena where everybody can come, from my two-year-old child to my 88-year-old grandmother. They can all have a great but different type of day, they all feel safe and secure, they all hopefully spend a reasonable amount of money, but most importantly: out of that comes a huge sense of connection with the event and a huge amount of passion.

What will the typical stadium of the future look like?
Up till now stadia were not much more then just simple concrete bowls with a bad reputation: a barren place of raw concrete and steel, which is used perhaps twenty times a year and lies idle about 90% of its life. When you go you are willing to ignore the fact that it is a very unpleasant place, as you have usually paid a lot of money to get in and you want to enjoy yourself. So you are prepared to put up with a lot of queuing in the toilets, and the fact that it will take you half an hour to buy a beer. These inconveniences are not going to be acceptable in the future. The whole idea is to design stadia that can compete with cinemas, shopping centres, airports, all the modern buildings of which we expect a certain level of comfort. To provide this comfort inside stadia we need to keep the weather out and therefore we need to close them. The whole trend of opening and closing roofs has developed because of this and it will become more and more normal. Instead of simple concrete bowls which were rather dominated by engineers, this new breed of buildings is very much dominated by architects. Engineers have had their go in producing big engineering statements with very little inside. There is still a certain client group that likes the icon building, a building that stands up in front of everybody and shouts. The modern stadia of the future will be all about the facilities that are packed into and around them and the effects these facilities have on their local environment. They are becoming buildings that are not just places where you go to, watch an event and go home. These buildings are becoming sophisticated, flexible and multi-use, therefore they will be used 40 or 50

times a year instead of 20 times. The Olympic Stadium in Australia we completed earlier this year, has only been open for about 8 months and has had 600 events already. Not only on the pitch, but also in the banqueting halls and the concourses. Where in your city do you put a building that is going to be used every day? Right in the middle. Stadia have become important building blocks around city centres and particularly in terms of regenerating parts of cities that have fallen into disrepair. They are being used as a magnet to bring people back into that part of the city. So I think stadia are becoming much more urban buildings. They are less about structural expressionism, they are more about fitting into the fabric of a city. They have to fulfil the same aesthetic and design criteria as any other city centre building.

Is public space an important subject in stadium design nowadays?
I think that stadia fulfil a very special requirement these days. We don't gather in our city plaza to hear what the king's edict is these days. There is really no occasion where a community comes together as a group other than a sporting event. So these buildings, although they have got a very strong financial image in terms of high technology, Internet and television, fulfil an incredibly important role in society because they make you feel that you have some kind of a connection to the rest of society. When that Mexican wave goes around, everybody rises and unites as if they are saying, 'I am part of the group, I am with you'. The strangers that were sitting next to you, you've been having great fun with for those couple of hours. Stadia bring us back to those community roots that we all miss a little. And if we ever loose that feeling, I think it would be a sad day. So public space to me is the bowl or the building itself. Public space is not necessarily that big open plaza outside it.

Intervie

Kisho K

'Architecture is a symbiosis of g

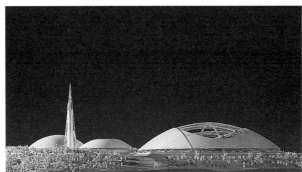

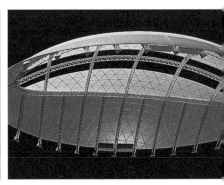

1   2

During the 1960s Kisho Kurokawa was one of the leading architects of the Metabolist movement. Since then he has become well-known for his theoretical-philosophical writings and has expanded his practice, including abroad. Recently he completed the extension to the Van Gogh Museum in Amsterdam.

Kisho Kurokawa: Our office is currently building two stadia that will be finished in 2001, the Oita Main Stadium and the Toyota City Stadium. The two have something in common: both of them have a capacity of 45,000 people and both are all-weather stadia, with a roof that can be opened and shut. For the rest they are very much different. This has to do with the sports for which the stadia have been designed: Oita Main Stadium is a stadium for both athletic sports and soccer (football), while Toyota City Stadium is specially designed for soccer games and other ball games. It also has to do with the different nature of the location. The total building site of Oita Stadium is so enormous that in the future an indoor swimming pool and a multi-purpose gymnasium will also be added. On the other hand, the Toyota Stadium has a limited building site. Therefore, instead of using the arch construction method, it was built using a construction with a roof hanging from four huge masts, which is more suitable for a small location.

What is the biggest challenge in the design of a stadium?
Being an architect, I concentrate all my efforts on the creation of a project, no matter what the subject of the building is. However, there are a few challenges that are particular to a stadium. I think the biggest challenges are:
1. To design a space that has a sense of unity for both players and audience.
2. To fulfil the requirement that the turf of the soccer field has to be exposed to the sun.
3. To make a stadium with an automatically opening and closing roof so that it can be used for multiple purposes after it is built.
4. In order to cater to the multi-media generation, we have to accommodate the (mobile) cameras that broadcast to the whole world and journalists' seats with computer terminals.
5. The smooth flow of a huge audience and an efficient evacuation system.

How do you think the stadium will evolve in the future?
In order to provide 'comfort' for the players and 'comfort' for the audience at the same time, a roof that can be opened and shut will become a must for stadia.
    A more dynamic picture for broadcast is now needed in a stadium because there is a concern not only for the audience who come for the game in the stadium, but also

w with

rokawa

al standards and local culture.'

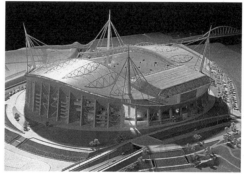

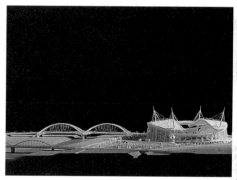

4   5   6

for the audience who watches the game in real-time via mass media. In the Oita Main Stadium there is a rail specially designed for a high-speed running-camera along the main arch. It is the first setting in the world that can capture the view from right above the athletes and also keep pace with them. This is one way of ensuring a dynamic picture. The number of people who watch sports will increase, and the stadium is becoming the place where people watch the games on television. That is, people go to the stadium to watch a real-time broadcast rather than the real game. Therefore we cannot ignore the trend whereby people are gathering together in stadia to watch games via a huge screen.

Multi-functionality is one of the conditions for smooth management of a stadium. This will be stimulated by progress in the technology of sound effects and light effects. In order to be multi-functional, the stadium needs a capacity of more than 45,000 spectators and an openable roof.

The stadium of the future will be of the all-weather type. In order to function well, the structure of an openable roof will have to be such that it can be opened and shut in a short period of time (around 30 minutes). An artificial turf, which resembles very closely a natural lawn, will be developed too, and will have to be officially approved.

1-4. Oita Main Stadium in Oita, 2001

5-6. Toyota City Stadium in Toyota City, 2001

Do you think there is a big difference in the design of sports buildings between Asia and Europe?
In sports, there are international operational groups and common rules to follow which means that there are a lot of common points for sports buildings, much more than for other kinds of buildings. But after all, architecture is a symbiosis of global standards and local culture, it reflects the culture of its country or the environment of the specific place it belongs to. Abstraction and geometry is a universal architectural language for the world. We can use this common language to create poetry in space. This is an expression of the space that reflects the local atmosphere. In Oita Main Stadium, the low profile of the sphere is a reflection of the surrounding mountains. The Toyota Stadium connects to my other project in Toyota City, the Toyota suspension bridge. The stadium has a hanging roof on four huge pillars. The suspension structure is a common building language. However, in Toyota City, where the main industry is car production, it also symbolises the mechanism that is used in cars.

Other uses

top: Toronto SkyDome fitted out as a powerboat showroom

bottom: Toronto SkyDome as arena for the Demolition De[r]

200

p: Hard rock concert in the Lenin Stadium in Moscow

bottom: Amnesty International rally

top: Opening ceremony of World Youth Festival, Pyongyang, South Korea

bottom: Roman Catholic mass in the Toronto SkyDon

top: 'De Kuip' in Rotterdam as location for wedding photos

bottom: Toronto SkyDome stages the opera Aida

The favourite stadium of... *Ted Troost*
haptonomist

'Chelsea's Stamford Bridge stadium is my favourite. The synergy between the players and the spectators has always been important for me. You have to be able to taste the players, and that is only possible in a stadium where there is hardly any distance between the players and the spectators. This is the case with the new section that they built at Chelsea, and that is why it has such a big effect on the atmosphere. The addition of a cinder track between the pitch and the public, on the other hand, has a chilling effect on stadia: these stadia are actually doomed to fail.'

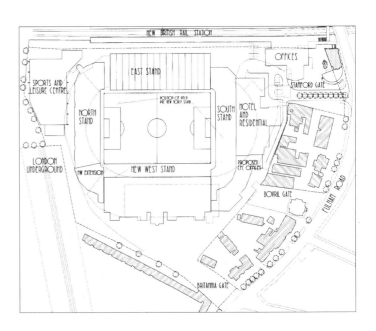

Mart Smeets
sports journalist and ex-basketball player

'The Yankees Stadium in the Bronx in New York is my favourite. It is old, it smells great, there are no skyboxes, and everybody there loves baseball. You have to take the subway to get there, and then you walk with all your fellow fans through New York's worst ghetto. The stadium was built in 1923 and it still functions perfectly; the acoustics are formidable. The stadia they are building now, for example the Amsterdam ArenA, are really horrendous.'

Part
of
nature

Stadio de Atletismo

name: Stadio de Atletismo
place: Madrid, Spain
date of construction: 1994
architects: Antonio Cruz and Antonio Oriz
with Jesús Ulargui
capacity: 20,500

On a barren plateau outside Madrid, Cruz and Ortiz designed a monumental concrete sculpture. Only the two flanking light masts give any hint that this is in fact an athletics stadium. In the not too distant future the stadium will be part of an extensive sports complex in which the striking grandstand will form an important point of reference. The relationship with the city is established by the spectacular view of the Madrid skyline from the stand and the panorama terrace.

The stadium consists of a 360-metre-long plateau containing a sunken athletics track and playing field. It is surrounded by simple terraces: three grassy slopes that recall the amphitheatres of ancient Greece. With all ancillary spaces, such as changing rooms, press rooms and an indoor practice area, located under-ground, the silhouette of the main structure acquires enormous visual impact.

The grandstand structure – which has earned the stadium the nickname 'the Spanish comb' – consists of obliquely placed double beams of reinforced concrete supported on the low side by a base course. The entrances to the stadium are tucked away in the gaps between the three gigantic perforated concrete walls that make up the building's façade. Because the design gives priority to the spectacular visual impact of the grandstand, the stadium is open to the skies, although a roof would not have been an unnecessary luxury in a climate where sweltering summers alternate with freezing winters.

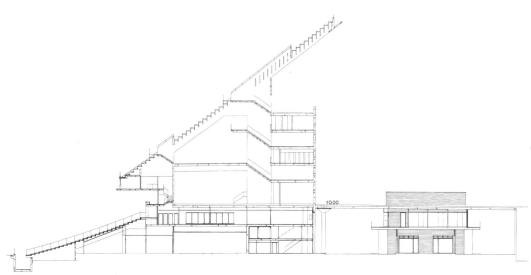

Nagano Olympic Memorial Arena

name: Nagano Olympic Memorial Arena
place: Nagano, Japan
date of construction: 1998
architects: Kajima Design Corporation with
Kume Sekkei & HOK
capacity: 10,000

What makes this indoor skating rink, nestled between the mountain ridges of the 'Japanese Alps', so much a part of its environment is not so much its outward appearance as the chosen techniques and constructions. The building is designed to be durable and to satisfy climatological requirements without resorting to complex technical systems.

The shape of the stadium, the materials, the construction and the appointments are all geared to this. On top of a concrete structure rests a wooden roof whose distinctive shape achieves savings on heating and ventilation. Natural ventilation and light are able to penetrate the overlapping sections of the ceiling.

Huge glass walls on the short sides provide views out over a park that was made possible by accommodating all the parking spaces underneath the building where they also serve as an insulating layer. There are wide exits for safe and speedy evacuation, even when it is snowing.

The building represented a big change compared with the earlier dome model with which Kajima had made its name; it is a linear, multi-purpose space that can be made bigger or smaller depending on the event, with the aid of movable stands.

Regardless of what sport is being played here, the audience is always close to the action.

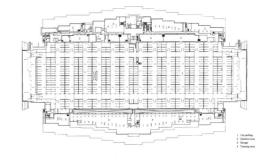

1 Car parking
2 Machine room
3 Storage
4 Training room

B1F plan S= 1/800

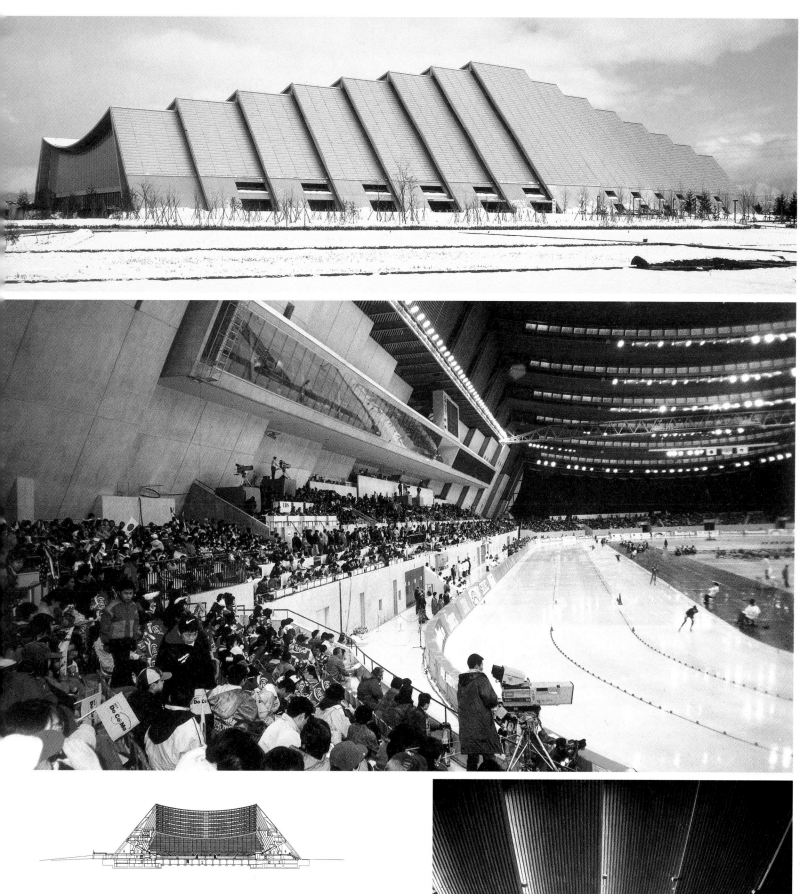

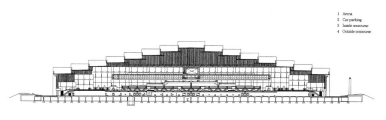

1 Arena
2 Car parking
3 Inside concourse
4 Outside concourse

Olympia-stadion

name: Olympiastadion
place: Munich, Germany
date of construction: 1965-1972
architects: Günter Behnisch and Frei Otto
capacity: 74,000

The stadium itself is fairly orthodox but the tent-roof construction by architect Frei Otto is so spectacular that the Olympic Stadium is among the most beautiful in the world. The typical German parkland setting also plays a part in this. Arranged among the trees and lakes in the rolling landscape of Olympic Park, stand not only the stadium but also an indoor pool, a gymnastics arena, a velodrome and a 275-metre-high Olympic Tower. The Olympic Village, where Arab terrorists murdered two Israeli athletes and held nine others hostage, stands on the edge of the complex.

This stadium has witnessed the high and low points of Dutch football. Both the unsuccessful World Cup final against Germany in 1974 and the successful European Cup final against the Soviet Union in 1988 were played under this high-tech Bedouin tent. The roof of translucent plexiglas suspended from eight cable-stayed masts, undulates above the west side of the stadium, gradually tapering off towards the sides. Two lighting units are attached to the edge; on the unroofed side the lights are placed on top of masts. The same roof construction was used for the swimming pool and the sports hall, producing a rolling landscape of 75,000 square metres of tent-like roof that is clearly intended to blend with the surrounding hills.

The oval stadium is partially buried so that only the raised grandstand projects above ground level. It is a fairly conventional concrete stand, supported on columns and transverse beams of the same material. The stadium may be surmounted by a superb canopy but when it rains this wonderful structure keeps barely 34 per cent of the spectators dry.

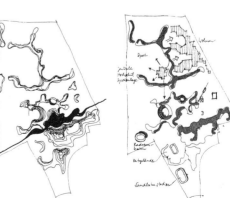

Stadium Australia

name: Stadium Australia
place: Sydney, Australia
date of construction: 1996-1999
architects: HOK + LOBB
capacity: 110,000

The Olympic Games being staged in Sydney in 2000 will go down in history as 'the Green Games'. The stadium, other sporting facilities and the Olympic Village have been designed as part of the Homebush and Homebush Bay parks. This ambitious plan – the transformation of a 760-hectare industrial site and rubbish tip into a park landscape – is based on a masterplan involving literally hundreds of town planners, architects, landscape architects, designers and artists. During, but above all after, the Olympic Games this new district will become Sydney's foremost recreation park. The actual Olympic site is very compactly built within a forty kilometre radius. It is hoped that this, together with an extensive public transport network, will drastically reduce car use. From the surrounding park landscape 'green fingers' in which infrastructure and public space are interwoven will penetrate deep into the ceremonial heart.

In the designs for the arenas only environmentally friendly and recyclable materials have been used, the stadia are naturally ventilated and so constructed as to take full advantage of natural daylight. The grass in the Olympic Stadium is irrigated with rainwater collected on the roof and stored in underground tanks.

The stadium has been designed around a sports field plus athletics track. The side stands are covered with a transparent roof. At the front the roofs are supported by a 295-metre-long arch while the back rests on the stands. After the Games the second tiers of the end stands will be demolished after which these stands, too, will be roofed over. The stadium, which will then hold 80,000 people, can be easily adapted for various sporting events. The lowest tier has been set on rails so that the stands can be moved for different sports, thus ensuring that the spectators are always close to the action.

Stadion Kirova

Name: Stadion Kirova
place: St. Petersburg, Russia
date of construction: 1938-1950
architect: unknown
capacity: 75,000

Located at the western tip of Krestovsky Island and surrounded on three sides by the Gulf of Finland, the Kirov Stadium seems like the furthermost point of the Russian empire. The stadium terminates the long axis of Victory Park which gives access to the stadium via a monumental flight of steps. The steps are flanked by neoclassical colonnades that centre on a statue of Kirov, one-time leader of the Leningrad Communist Party.

The design is not much more than an oval crater containing a football pitch and an athletics track. The stands ascend in a single movement and are a long way from the playing field. All spectator positions are open to the skies and, as usual in socialist stadia, all are seats. Nonetheless, the Communist Party does have its own separate terrace in the western stand.

The location is not without consequences for the stadium's use. Until the

1930s, Krestovsky Island was a marsh in the Neva estuary and occasionally, when the sea level in the Gulf of Finland rises, it reverts to this situation. At such times the stadium is inaccessible and unusable. The northern location also means that the stadium is regularly cut off by an expanse of ice or buried under a thick layer of snow. As a result the stadium is only playable from mid-June to October and the home team, Zenit Leningrad, is frequently obliged to switch to the Lenin Sport and Concert Centre, an indoor hall with a capacity of 19,500 and a pitch of artificial grass.

Itäkeskus Swimming pool

name: Itäkeskus Swimming pool
place: Helsinki, Finland
date of construction: 1987-1991
architects: Arkkitehtitoimisto Hyvämäki
Karhunen Parkkinen

At the foot of a pine-covered hill in Helsinki stands a modest entrance building that gives no inkling of what is immediately beneath the ground: a gigantic hole carved out with explosives and drill borers has been fitted out as an 'aquatic paradise'. In addition to a 50-metre-long swimming pool there is a jacuzzi with a star-spangled sky-ceiling, a children's pool, saunas with sunbeds, in short a complete underground amusement complex. All these spaces have been hacked out around a central granite column 16 x 26 metres thick. Savings on scarce space, energy costs and maintenance were the main reasons for going underground. Some 320,000 people a year swim their lengths here under the rough-hewn stone ceiling.

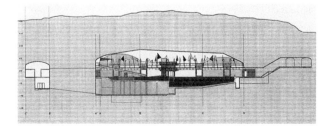

Intervie

HI

'These buildings reflect the

1   2   3

HNTB (Howard, Needles, Tammen & Bergendorff) was founded in 1914 in Kansas City, Missouri. Sports architecture is one of the many studios within the office. Starting in the late sixties more attention was given to sports design and in 1979 a number of architects were hired from the Kansas City firm of Devine James Labinski Myers. These all left in 1983 to form HOK Sport; another group left in 1989 to form Ellerbe Becket Sports Group

Can you explain the different approaches to a baseball park, football stadium or an arena?
Tad L. Shultz (senior designer sports architecture): In the sixties and seventies they put both baseball and football in one building, which means that you have to compromise both of those geometries, a square and a rectangle. From the late eighties on we have seen the growth of the economics of sport to the extent that each team now is getting their own field, for example Camden Yards (HOK) which was one of the first baseball-only facilities. Baseball has a very long history of 150 years, so when new ballparks are done the design constantly goes back into history. Football doesn't have that. Football really came to fruition in the late fifties when it was put in old baseball parks. In the sixties and seventies they put football and baseball together in multi-purpose stadia and only very recently has football by itself

been considered as a building type. Football has its own new style to find. So you can have a tailored football stadium, a tailored baseball stadium and there are no compromises involved.

Can you discuss the recent developments in American stadia?
Shultz: In America there has been a fundamental shift on who goes to our professional sports games. It used to be families, but now it is more single and unmarried adults and corporations, because the cost of going to a game for a family has almost driven that market away. For a family of four to go and see the Boston Red Sox play is almost 200 dollars. So most of the people who purchase the packages, the suites and the clubs, are corporations and groups, because they can afford it. Our stadia used to be named after public leaders, famous presidents, politicians who had influence on getting the buildings done, now those names are sold into naming rights and they are sold to the highest bidder and those are corporations. Every arena, major league facility or NFL facility is named after corporations who purchase long-term lease packages to have their name painted on the building. It has driven all the prices up, it is a vicious circle.

Timothy G. Cahill (vice president – director of design): It's

w with

TB

iety which they are serving'

4

5

6

7

really starting to affect design as well. We have been asked to look at ways to introduce the flexibility of naming a specific gate for a specific match or event. The design of the stadia and the use of technology to accommodate that is something that we have to take into account. It's just because the players and the teams have become so expensive that the owners are looking for ways for these facilities to generate more income than they have ever done before.

In Europe stadia are tending to become more multi-functional, so different people will visit these buildings. What's happening with the multi-use in America?

Shultz: In the early nineties we saw the beginning of 'entertainment design'. The idea was to not only have sports there, but as many event days as possible. For baseball that is extremely difficult, because baseball has a very strange configuration and is open-air, whereas many football stadia are enclosed and are more symmetrical. Arenas are even completely enclosed so they have the most flexibility. We saw an explosion of entertainment design – from concerts to floating shows – that could maximize 20,000 seats in an arena or 70,000 seats in a football stadium. It has had varying degrees of success. Howe-

1. Extension of Commonwealth Stadium in Lexington (Kentucky), 1999

2. Kemper Arena in Kansas City (Missouri), 1997

3. New Mile High Stadium in Denver (Colorado), 2001

4. Renovation of Oakland Arena in Oakland (California), 1997

5. Renovation of Ohio Stadium in Columbus (Ohio), 2001

6. Louisville Slugger Field in Louisville (Kentucky), 2000

7. Raley Field in West Sacramento (California), 2000

ver, it is all geared toward maximizing the facility that is so expensive to use. We have very few solely privately funded stadia, it is a share between public and private. This means you continually have to justify the huge expenses. The more the owners can show the stadium as a community resource, the more they will have the support of the public when it comes to a referendum in their city. The entertainment design really was born out of helping justify the cost of these huge buildings.

But what does this shift imply for the organization of the stadium?
Cahill: The amenities and packages like the clubs and seating are getting much larger. They sell suite and club packages in varying forms as a way to market the stadium. It becomes a symbol for corporate and civic pride, and the corporations want to invest in their community that way. So for these owners to be competitive, they need to make new facilities. I have often wondered if sports architecture would slow down in this country, or around the globe for that matter, but I think it is going in the opposite direction. People are using the entertainment venues as a release more than they ever have. We're seeing it in the minor league level and the collegial level, large amounts of

dollars being spent on these facilities to ensure that the entertainment option remains.

Shultz: America is an entertainment society. Every year our movies break box office records. We always look for entertainment, and our culture is such that we will always continue to support sports. The minor league stadia in America have doubled in the last fifteen years, which is really incredible. Then there is the collegial and international market and unlike Amsterdam, Paris or London who do a national stadium, our cities all have three or four stadia. The number of projects in the United States is enormous. Literally every fifteen to twenty years the sport reinvents its own economics and the buildings are part of the economics of that sport. So it is hard to see the cycle ever stopping.

Does a stadium reflect the attitude to sport these days?
Shultz: I think the building reflects the society which it is serving. In the thirties, forties and fifties, you could take your child to a ballpark and it would cost you only three or four dollars to go. There weren't club and suite amenities, it was simply an intimate place to go and see a game and our culture was like that. It was located in the downtown core, because these were pre-war times. When everybody came back from the war you saw this big urban flight to the suburbs and 90% of the stadia built during that time started to go suburban. We had the modernist movement throughout the country in terms of architecture and the stadia reflected that very monumental design – fixed circular spaceships in the middle of a parking lot. They were reflecting what was going on in that age of architecture and they were suburban located, they weren't contextual because America was leaving the downtown core. And now you see at the end of the century that we redevelop our downtowns, we understand that they are a resource and we combine all of those things now. We know that we want to bring back some of the intangible sentiment to our stadia that they used to have, but we are also in the nineties where money and technology rules. We are learning now how to merge all those things together in a huge building with a retractable roof and 150 suites, located in the downtown area of a city. Things with an incredible technology that continue to expand and grow each year and I think it is a direct reflection of our culture whether it is 1940, 1960 or the year 2000.

Façade

Olympia-stadion

name: Olympiastadion
place: Berlin, Germany
date of construction: 1933-1936
architect: Werner March
capacity: 76,000

Many stadia are symbols of power and that is certainly the case with Berlin's Olympic Stadium, the design of which was closely supervised by Adolf Hitler. He saw the 1936 Olympics as an excellent opportunity to impress the world with his might. The resulting neo-classical temple of sport is supported by over one hundred limestone columns expressive of 'invincible German strength and the enduring might of National Socialism'. The open stadium had two tiers of seating. The first tier was below ground level and on its south side it contained the seats of honour and a special box for the

Führer. The oval plan form took its cue from the shape of the athletics track.

The stadium was part of the 131 hectare Reichs-sportfeld which contained a swimming pool, various playing fields and an open-air amphitheatre for 20,000 spectators. To the west of the stadium was the Maiveld, an exercise ground the size of ten football pitches with stands on three sides. At the far side of the Maiveld, on the longitudinal axis of the stadium, stood a 75 metre-high tower, the Führerturm.

The Marathon Gate, an opening in the second tier of seating, provided the link between the stadium and the

exercise ground and a platform for the Olympic flame. On top of the two sturdy towers flanking the marathon gate are plaques bearing the names of all the gold medal winners, including that of black athlete Jesse Owens whose victory was a source of acute embarrassment to Hitler.

The stadium was thoroughly renovated for the 1974 World Cup. The north and south stands were roofed over: columns, which impede the spectators' view of the ground, support a steel space-frame structure covered with translucent plastic panels. These modern materials are in stark contrast with the sober design of Werner March.

erlin. Original-Fliegeraufnahme des Reichssportfeldes mit Dietrich-Eckart-Bühne

Wembley Stadium

name: Wembley Stadium
place: London, England
date of construction: 1922-1923
architects: J. Simpson and M. Ayrton
architects for renovation: Foster & Partners /
HOK+LOBB (The World Stadium Team)
capacity: 90,000

If England is the cradle of soccer, Wembley Stadium is the game's Mecca. Every year, tens of thousands of football fans make the pilgrimage to the sacred site where the English national team won its one and only world title in 1966.

British football stadia are characterized by a motley assemblage of extensions and new stands added over time. They are renowned for their unique atmosphere: the stands and terraces are so close to the pitch that the public is twelfth man. Wembley however, was built in one go and the pitch is separated from the stands by a greyhound race track. Nonetheless, it is the greyhound races that have so far saved Wembley from bankruptcy.

Wembley was built for the 1924 World's Fair as part of the British Empire Exhibition, an amusement park symbolizing the might and grandeur of the British Empire. The stadium was the radiant centrepiece of this display and its façades were in the style of an oriental palace with the famous Twin Towers as trademark. Like the Empire itself, the Exhibition went into rapid decline; only great ingenuity saved Wembley Stadium from a similar fate.

The famous Twin Towers will soon disappear for ever when the antiquated stadium is replaced by a high-tech design by The World Stadium Team. A steel arch, 133 metres high, will take over the visually definitive role of the towers. The new façade follows the model of the old stadium and consists of a glazed front elevation between two side jetties. The stands run all around the ground and the seats will be accessed by lifts. The roof will be movable in order to guarantee optimal sunlighting for the grass and optimal protection for the spectators.

89 Soldier Field & Field Museum
A Century of Progress
Chicago 1933 World's Fair

Soldier Field

name: Soldier Field
place: Chicago, United States
date of construction: 1918-1924
architect: unknown
capacity: 66,944

The design of Soldier Field is based on the U-shaped Circus Maximus in Rome built in the first century AD. The form, the façades and the monumental, classical architecture is typical of the huge stadia that were built in America in this period. The design called for the stadium to terminate in two pillars topped by flames commemorating the dead of First World War dead. Instead of this, a neo-classical structure was built complete with colonnades that serve as a hall of honour. The stands are crowned by two more colonnades between which most of the ground's 116 hospitality boxes are located.

The stadium, home to the Chicago Bears (American football) and Chicago Fire (soccer), is gigantic and the distance between the seating in the stands and the playing field is so great that many spectators must have difficulty making out the players on the field, never mind the ball.

Olympisch Stadion

name: Olympisch Stadion
place: Amsterdam, the Netherlands
date of construction: 1927-1928
architect: Jan Wils
capacity: 34,155
extension: 1937
architect: Jan Wils
capacity: 65,000
restoration: 1998-1999
architect: André van Stigt

The brick façade of the Olympic Stadium reveals the influence of Frank Lloyd Wright: in the concrete elements incorporated into the façade (the flower boxes flanking the entrances and the cantilevered canopies) and the strong horizontal line.

Behind the elegant façade there lurks a thoroughly functional stadium. The playing field was originally encircled by an athletics track and beyond that a 500-metre-long cycle track. The stands conformed to the shape of this cycle track. Wils designed curved terraces to match the curve at either end. Along the straight sides he designed two 60-metre-long covered stands, in the west a grandstand, and in the east a 'marathon' stand containing the marathon gate.

The stadium had a harmonious horizontality (with only the grandstand projecting above the rest) punctuated by the vertical accent of the marathon tower. This 42.195 metre-high tower was topped by a shallow bowl for the Olympic flame.

In 1937 the stadium was modified so that it could compete with Rotterdam's Feyenoord Stadium. The height of the stands behind the goals was raised by the addition of two concrete rings which destroyed the horizontality and obscured the brick façade.

Now the dilapidated and outdated stadium has been restored under the direction of André van Stigt. In future it will be used as an athletics stadium. Modern requirements – eight tracks rather than the six used in 1928 and straight sprint tracks along each side – meant that there was no room for the cycle track. The space beneath the stands has been converted to offices which have a superb view of the action via a large glass wall. The main intervention was the removal of the concrete ring added in 1937. The fine brick façade has been restored to public view.

The favourite stadium of...

Ronald en Frank de Boer
professional football players

Ronald de Boer: 'Nou Camp in Barcelona is the most beautiful stadium, especially since it doesn't have a roof. It has a big pitch that isn't surrounded by fences or ditches, which means that the spectators can sit really close.'
Frank de Boer: 'Every stadium should look like the Nou Camp stadium in Barcelona. It is a great stadium for the spectators, with no fences or ditches. It seems as if the supporters could simply walk right onto the pitch. It is a great big stadium with a spacious pitch. The changing rooms are spacious and still have their original features.'

Bettine Vriesekoop
former table-tennis champion

'The most beautiful stadium I have ever seen is Nou Camp in Barcelona. In 1985 I won the Top 12 in a neighbouring sports hall. As you walk into the stadium, you are overcome by its enormity: it is very impressive, and there is a wonderful pitch.'

Interview with
Ellerbe Becket
'You don't want your investment in a stadium to be a one-liner'

1   2   3

Ellerbe Becket is one of the oldest architectural firms in the United States. In 1909 Franklin Ellerbe founded an architectural practice in St. Paul, Minnesota. In 1933, the Becket firm was established in Los Angeles. Ellerbe Becket is the result of a merger between these two offices in 1988. In that same year the Ellerbe Becket Sports Group was launched by five former employees of HNTB. The office is head-quartered in Kansas City, Missouri and is nowadays considered to be the world leader in building arenas.

What are the current developments in the United States compared to Europe?
Bill Johnson (director of design): I think the situation here is unique to the world. Everywhere else stadia tend to be symbols of civic pride, symbols of countries. The way the Olympics were done in Barcelona for example is very different from the way the Olympics were done here.

1. Washington State Football/Soccer Stadium (with exhibition space), Seattle (Washington), 2002

2. National Car Rental Center in Fort Lauderdale (Florida), 1998

3. Bank One Ballpark, Phoenix (Arizona), 1998

Especially in Asia, but also in Western Europe, they seem to have a lot of government money. The buildings here are usually financed with a partnership between the owners of the team and some tax money that is grudgingly given up by the taxpayers. Whereas the international stadia may be monuments, the American buildings are very practical, pragmatic and based completely on revenue generation. A client who owns the Phoenix Suns Basketball Team, has said to me more then once, 'Every dollar that I spend on this project better realize some amount of profit in return.'

We design the buildings for generating revenue, advertising opportunities, sponsorship opportunities and naming rights opportunities. The building has to provide an excellent fan experience, but it also has to provide the balance of creating the money. So I think the US model is much different. Stadia in Europe don't seem to focus on generating revenue, other than ticket sales. I don't see the Stade de France having naming rights. Naming rights alone in a stadium could be worth from 30 to a 100 million dollars.

David Murphy (principal): The dollar is the bottom-line in all of our facilities. The challenge for us is to meld the economic reality of these facilities with excellent design. In a lot of American facilities the design is more an engineering solution or design is not a priority. In Europe there is more flexibility to create cost-effectively elegant structures. Whereas here rules for safety are so great that sometimes our structures become very clunky; or if you would make them very elegant they would be very expensive. There is more freedom in architecture in Europe. Some facilities are pure architectural statements.

But visiting the Stade de France was surprised about the lack of functional facilities. It is a beautiful building, but it would never work here. Toilets or other fan amenities that are major revenue components to these buildings in the United States don't exist in Europe. One of our clients taught us early on that if you don't have enough restrooms, people won't buy beverages. Human nature takes over.

Does a stadium represent the attitudes to sport at the time that it was built?
Johnson: We believe that a building should be built with modern materials, that it should be reflective of the kind of

a big hacienda. There was a real backlash amongst the owners because they felt like that was a real cliché. People are looking for something a bit more substantial. You don't want your investment in a stadium to be a one-liner.

What was good about the retro building was that it broke out of the sort of low-finished, low-expectation kind of concrete boxes or bunkers that we were building. But where it has gone to is I think kind of unfortunate. Owners see a facility and they realize the economic model that it has created and they want the same building. We believe that our buildings are unique to each owner. We really push our ownership to say you don't want to do something just because somebody else did it, you want something that is unique, as a personality is unique to you.

You just said that retro and amusement are things from the past. What else?
Johnson: I would say that the amusement is not so much the past. Do you know the term Disneyfication? We use that term a lot. The Disneyfication of architecture is not about building timeless, solid quality buildings, it is about creating a stage set. The buildings are build out of Styrofoam and spread with plaster and big cornices, ribbons and bows. Applied to the stadium it was all about making people want to come for things other than the game. The game was just part of the whole day experience and that entertainment aspect is fine, but what happened was that the people that really loved the sport were going to say that their football team or

4

5

technology that exists in the building industry and it should be representative of the people that built it and the time and place that it was built. Many of the multi-purpose buildings that are being torn down now were a product of the late-modern cold and generic architecture that was happening in the 1960s and the 1970s. They tended to represent our building industry. There was a real backlash against that when Camden Yards (HOK) was built, the baseball park in Baltimore. This building is like a movie set with old brick arches and green steel. It was the beginning of retro buildings, buildings that look like old buildings but have all the new materials that people demand on the inside. It was a time when everything wanted to be an amusement park. There were some proposals out there that really went over the top. One design for a potential NFL-team in Los Angeles was in the form of

4. Bank One Ballpark, Phoenix (Arizona), 1998

5. Conseco Fieldhouse, Indianapolis (Indiana), 1999

6. Bank One Ballpark, Phoenix (Arizona), 1998

baseball team was lost in all this junk. The pendulum swings and is swinging back to a place where there is a nice balance between things that are sports related, but still work within the context of going to see a soccer match or a baseball game.

Virtual reality is one of the new trends. How much do you take this into account when you design a stadium?
Johnson: Especially here in the Mid West the people are crazy about American football. The football game is just one tiny bit of a day-long event.
When they wake up in the morning they pack their cars and their coolers with food, probably more elaborate than any kind of dinner they have had all week long, they take their barbecues and they head off on the road. They get to the parking lots, they stake out their territory, they

erect tents and scaffolding, they put big flags on and put their cooking gear out. Then they bring their food out and the beer. All this is three or four hours before the game starts, then all of their friends start to come, and some people even pull their vans up with televisions sets so they can see the pre-game activities. On the other side you have all the VIP sponsorship tents. It's like a circus of tents with all the media sponsors inviting their corporate guests. They have catered affairs and drinks. Everyone goes into the game, they have this incredible experience and they start all over again after the game and do this till the sun goes down.

You can talk about virtual reality, there are always going to be those people that don't want to leave their house, but for some people this is the one thing. Even if it is almost beyond their means in terms of affording the ticket. They do it with a passion and the NFL is in these cases absolutely smart enough to capitalize on this and realize that they can do things to make that experience better by putting facilities out on the parking lots like hook-ups and electricity power. They organize entertainment on the plaza areas, so they start to feed on it and create a sort of festival atmosphere. You'll never get that sitting in your living room even if you have a big flat screen.

3

Power and control

top: Pinochet's prisoners in Chili, 1973

bottom: Feyenoord supporte

top: Galgenwaard dismantled by home team supporters after the final match, Utrecht 1981   bottom: 'Ditch' at Feyenoord Stadium

top: Nazi supporters applaud Hitler in the Nuremberg Stadium, 11 September 1938

bottom: Nike chairman and founder, Phil Kni

top: Incident during cup final between Ajax and PSV, Rotterdam, 17 May 1998

bottom: Jorien van den Herik and Ronald Koeman

During the war the stadium was right on the front
line. Close by, yet inaccessible. On both sides the men
shuffled around it, starving. Deprived of football all
they could do was to think back on the matches that had
been fought out there, and in the remembering the local derbies
in particular became veritable pitched battles.

Men without football are sentimental. On my first visits to
the city, when it was still under siege, they would often make
me stop and look back over their shoulder with them. There,
in the middle of a heavily bombarded district, was the stadium,
they said. It lay in a bowl between the hills and the lighting
masts had been torn down, so from where we stood it was
invisible. But they wanted me to look all the same. They
themselves had played there in the juniors or had shouted
from the terraces. They talked about it as if their stories
might bring it to them. Nowhere have I felt so keenly how
frustrating that is, a football pitch no one may use, a city
that cannot get to its stadium.

Zeljo-Sarajevo 1-2

Chris Keulemans

Now I'm on my way to the local derby. It is a sunny spring day. Beside me in the taxi is Senad Pecanin, a huge bear of a man, a journalist and sports addict. We drive past the long, concrete housing blocks of Grbavica, an ugly name that during the war, when the Serbians were in control there, was uttered wistfully by the same men who now walk, clad in blue-and-white and singing, past the withered flowerbeds from which the mines have yet to be cleared. It is almost four years since Dayton but there is still a sense of triumph in being able to walk and drive freely along these streets. Senad hangs out of the window and greets his comrades in passing.

Opposite a block of flats whose staircase was brought to its knees by a direct hit early in the war, stands the stadium. Broad-shouldered young men, some still with the unfocused gaze of the veteran, mill around the ticket booth and the cigarette kiosks. Then a loud shout goes up. Here come the red-and-whites, marching in formation from the city, yelling and hooting. They turn to the left and enter the stadium at the side.

Senad explains it all to me. Red is Sarajevo, the team of the nouveau riches: fellow townsmen to be sure, but the kind who don't care how they come by their money, not during the war and not now. Blue, that's us: Zeljeznicar, affectionately shortened to Zeljo. Once the club of the railway workers, still the darlings of the traditional city dwellers: those who stayed, even when the mortars were falling. Less money perhaps, poorer players, but none of that matters. Just so long as they win the derby. They have had to contain themselves for four long years. The rivalry is all the more murderous for that.

Behind the solid figure of Senad, I allow myself to be carried along with the mass of pushing, heaving male bodies to the covered terrace. The sight that greets us is timeless. Before us lies a grass pitch marked with white rectangles, the proportions of which are as familiar to people today as those of cathedrals once used to be. To the left, close to the pitch, the enclosures for the red opponents, armed with their horns and rattles. To the right a small, newly roofed grandstand for the dignitaries, and even a couple of wooden hospitality boxes. On the roof, standing in the wind, are two camera teams. And across from us the jubilant hard core of Zeljo supporters. Blue-and-white flags and fireworks beneath the scoreboard that contains nothing but the names of the two teams, the score, the clock and the national emblem. All restored to its original state: the simple light masts stick straight up into the air, the stands are of stone. Beyond them the hill rises up to a quarter with steep, winding streets. Some of the windows where the snipers crouched out of sight below the windowsill, their sights fixed on anything that moved around the forbidden shrine, are blackened still. Some of the houses are still roofless, others are in the throes of rebuilding. On the balconies and the new roofs stand men sporting blue-and-white scarves and caps. It could be anywhere. Anywhere where men fight and love football.

The football is mediocre and impassioned. Eager beavers, hogging the ball as if their lives depended on it.

Senad apologizes for the standard of play: most of the old players have either fled or returned injured from the front. After every foul they roll about on the ground, gesturing wildly, you would almost think: mortally wounded. As if the people in this city cannot tell the difference between real injuries and playacting. Teams of men with stretchers run on and off the pitch, sometimes two or three at the same time. The referee is stretched to the limit. The stands are in uproar. Red and blue bombard one another with chants. The red keeper, Mirsad Dedic, who is also keeper for the national team, is a showman and a shaven-headed demagogue. After every mistake by his defenders he storms out of goal, grabs their head in his huge gloves, shakes it furiously, cursing all the while, and then plants a kiss on it. Our enclosure rewards him with a barrage of insults in the best football tradition, as trite as they are inventive. Senad translates for me, in between the abuse. The things that should be done to Dedic's mother beggar all description. But as soon as the ball is out of his zone Dedic turns our way and returns the compliments with equal force. Our mothers too, and all at the same time!

We lose 2–1, quite unfairly of course. Three players have been sent off and even those in the grandstand are standing on the seats after the final whistle. I look at the blackened windows, up there on the hill. As so often in this city, I feel that since the first shots some boundary has been crossed that is still more or less intact in cities that have not known war. Aggression is allowed to take a direct, public form. They may not shoot any more, but violence is still only a short step away. No one has to keep up the appearance of civilization any more; everyone knows what went on here.

There is no false shame, least of all in a football stadium, where aggression is all in the game. They all hurl themselves shamelessly into the general frenzy. On the pitch the referee is cornered first by the blue players. Then he is set upon by the very police who should be rescuing him. Kicking policemen must in turn be dragged away from the referee and linesmen by soldiers. From the stands red and blue fans shout in unison, stabbing their fingers in the direction of the referee: Ubiti! Ubiti! Kill him! There's an insane sort of happiness in being able to scream blue murder here, where for years no one dared show their face.

Not a bit of it, says Senad in car going home, with the mild irony that has a way of turning life here on its head. I've got it all wrong. What we were shouting back there on the terrace was: u biti – let's think things over together. Let's consider the matter. Football in Sarajevo is philosophy, he explains, a game for thinkers. Not war. He looks at me in such a way that I no longer know what to believe, in this city where philosophers shoot one another and a perfectly ordinary derby can degenerate into a symposium.

The favourite stadium of... *Ole Bouman*

editor-in-chief, Archis

Sur place

Dressing room in the catacombs. The odours of fresh tyres, freshly-washed tricots, mentholated emollient. Skilled hands on shaved legs, nimbly kneading today's champion. New racing trousers, with a real chammy crotch. The shiny shirt glides out of the bag to fit sleek and skintight on the torso. Quick trip to the toilet. While relieving yourself you listen to the sounds from above, the drone of the large engines spinning.

Then the long walk through the bowels of the Olympic Stadium in Amsterdam. The clitter-clatter of the plates of cycling shoes on the concrete floor. The echo of volleys of laughter. A last-minute visit to 'the pill doctor' for the much-needed rest. All perfectly natural of course. He has some last-minute advice and repeats the inevitable mantra: 'It's all about the legs.' Providing you have the right mindset, of course.

Further. The bike is already upstairs. And then, all of a sudden, the light. That first glance: How many spectators are there? What is the atmosphere like? The stands are well filled. The smell of warm sausage. The wonderful movements of colourful little figures around the velodrome. The sun is already low in the sky and the floodlight masts throw their shadows across the stadium. First a nice little spin on the rollers to loosen up. Shudder at the sight of the turbo-thighs of your opponent. And meanwhile half-listen to the unstoppable prittle-prattle of the commentator. Ladies and gentlemen, a warm hand for our St. John's Ambulance man, Mr. Jones, without whom we would not be able to hold this cycling event. Of course, we hope that his services won't be necessary.

A sudden shriek of horror. A fall. Two racers tumble downward from the top of the track. Sheaves of grazed skin. Mr. Jones!!! And the muzak returns, courtesy of Brunobox & Co., Zaandam.

The bell goes. Gentlemen, to your places for the first heat of the sprint series. Attendants leap up to accompany you to the track. A few slaps on the thighs and face to get the circulation going. With the shoes now one with the bike, a quick shake of the calves. To your marks. Get set…

Then it begins. The start is almost imperceptible, at a snail's pace. To the top rim of the arena, gaining height on the bank, front wheel pushed to the side, legs flexed, standing on the pedals, hands secure in the curve of the handlebars. The bike scarcely moves. This is the real cycling. Sur place, a concentrated track stand high on the bank. At first all attention is focused on your opponent, you simply want to avoid setting

off from the lead position. Gradually the tension becomes more palpable. Hamstrings, neck and forearms under immense pressure. Utmost concentration. The opponent doesn't give an inch, and mirrors my moves.

Then the first cramp. Don't lose it now. The spectators, at first as quiet as mice intent on the spectacle, start to get restless. We've been standing like this for minutes, and the growing cheers and jeers bespeak a mixture of amused interest and impatience. 'Hey! You won't get the prize till you get to the finish,' one of the lads jokes. Hilarity.

It's taking too long. We see ourselves through the eyes of the spectators. Two cyclists, balancing carefully on a steep knife-edge. This isn't cycling, this is a circus. What if I lose my balance and fall? What a disgrace. I'm paying too much attention to those cramped legs and forearms; the other guy will simply fly past me later. And then there is another heat and perhaps even a ride-off. You can't imagine that the spectators would be so intrigued by two motionless cyclists.

The doubts build up. Until the thin line breaks. Then you are glad that you've held your position up high on the ban-

king. Just let yourself drop, gain speed, a catapult-like spurt towards…the beauty queen who kisses the winner.

Sculpture

Olympic Halls

Takamatsu Hall

name: Olympic Halls
place: Tokyo, Japan
date of construction: 1961-1964
architect: Kenzo Tange
capacity: 16,246 (big hall),
5,300 (small hall)

name: Takamatsu Hall
place: Takamatsu, Japan
date of construction: 1962
architect: Kenzo Tange
capacity: 2,500

In the two Olympic sports arenas Tange combined modern design with traditional Japanese forms. The buildings are characterized by a flowing line, an expressive treatment of concrete and above all by the eccentric roof construction: a concrete and steel tent roof in two versions. The suspended roof construction elaborates on the examples of the Philips pavilion by Le Corbusier, designed for the 1958 Brussels World's Fair, and Eero Saarinen's hockey stadium in New Haven (1958).

The larger hall contains a 50-metre pool and a diving pool. The plan is composed of two semicircles both of which have been extended at one end to create the entrance. The roof of steel sheets rests on steel cables suspended from two concrete columns. A central opening between the columns admits light (natural and artificial) to the arena.

The plan of the smaller hall, intended for boxing matches, is also based on a circle. An eccentrically placed column supports the roof which makes a spiralling movement. Both roofs are constructed to stand up to the tornado-force winds that are common in this area.

For pedestrians, the two stadia are linked by a raised walkway above the surprisingly small car park. On the other hand, the complex is flanked by two metro stations built specially for the 1964 Olympic Games.

Almost simultaneously with the Olympic halls, Tange built a small stadium in southern Japan. The building sits there like a concrete boat on four gigantic concrete 'blocks'. The actual hall stands on a substructure containing offices and service areas. The striking design is explicitly brutalist with rough, undressed concrete walls and deliberately out-of-proportion details such as windows and the water run-off. It demonstrates once again the virtuosity attained by the Japanese master in discovering an architectural language appropriate to concrete.

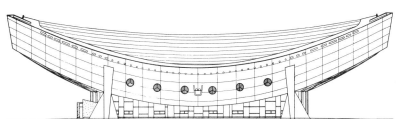

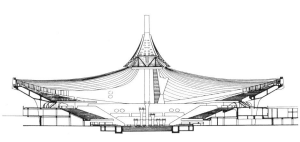

Cross section of the great stadium 1:1000

Querschnitt des großen Stadions

Coupe transversale sur le grand stade

Stadio Comunale

name: Stadio Comunale
place: Florence, Italy
date of construction: 1930-1932
architects: Pier Luigi Nervi
capacity: 49,033

Before the Second World War stadia were often designed as neoclassical palaces or the utilitarian construction was hidden away behind a stone or brick façade. The first architect to show that a modern stadium could also be built in a modern style, was Pier Luigi Nervi. His design for the Stadio Comunale in Florence strikes a balance between brute force and sculptural elegance. The concrete construction is fully revealed and dominates the architectural image of the stadium which was built for the 1934 World Cup. A major visual element is the staircase placed against the outside of the stadium. It consists of two opposing spirals and provides a light-hearted accent amidst the taut rhythm of the supporting structure. Soaring above the stands is a slender, 55-metre-high marathon tower. But the true power of Nervi's engineering art is most clearly demonstrated by the roofing. The distinctive shape of the enormous cantilever above the grand-stand is a direct expression of the underlying structural forces.

The stadium is asymmetrical in plan to accommodate the sprinting track on one side of the playing field. And because of the athletics track encircling the field, the distances between it and the spectators are enormous. Despite this lack of intimacy, the stadium was thoroughly renovated for the 1990 World Cup. The concrete was restored, the pitch lowered and extra stands were built along the long sides of the pitch. It was turned into an all-seater stadium and spectator facilities were upgraded. Its heritage status saved the antiquated and poorly appointed stadium from demolition.

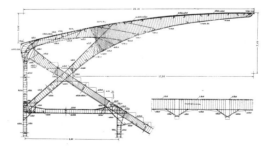

Firenze - Stadio Comunale

Stadio Flaminio Palazzetto dello Sport

name: Stadio Flaminio and
Palazzetto dello Sport
place: Rome, Italy
date of construction: 1957-1959
architects: Pier Luigi Nervi
with Antonio Nervi
capacity: 55,000 and 5,000

Twenty-five years after Nervi built the Stadio Comunale in Florence, he received another commission to design a stadium, this time for the 1960 Olympic Games in Rome. The Stadio Flaminio is a good deal smaller than the Florence stadium and it has no athletic track, but because of this it is far more inti-mate and better suited to football matches.

In terms of design it has a lot in common with its predecessor. The bowl of the stadium topped by stands is made of prefabri-cated elements with no attempt at finishing. This bowl is carried by a series of expressive, fork-shaped concrete supports. A distinctive feature is the public approach via a raised corridor under the shelter of the cantilevered stands. Here, too, the sculptural appearance of supports and roof is a direct expression of the forces played out in the structure.

The same is true of one of the sports halls that Nervi designed a stone's throw away from the stadium, the Palazzetto dello Sport. This is a central-plan structure capped by an enormous dome, a modern Pantheon where sportsmen and women are worshipped as gods. The dome is supported on 36 Y-shaped concrete columns, for all the world like dozens of people straining to hold up the roof.

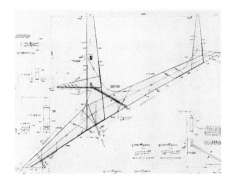

David S. Ingalls Hockey Rink

name: David S. Ingalls Hockey Rink
place: New Haven, United States
date of construction: 1956-1958
architect: Eero Saarinen
capacity: 3,000

This relatively small stadium on the campus of Yale University has a fairly complex form. Saarinen drew his inspiration from the dynamics of the game and the excitement of the sporting contest, renouncing the static stadium form in favour of a building that is the very incarnation of action and energy.

The building evokes associations with a Viking ship (complete with figurehead)

owing to the construction with a parabolic concrete supporting beam that runs like a backbone along the full length of the oval plan and guarantees the spectators an unimpeded view of the action. On the two shorter sides, the roof curls upwards to form the glazed entrances. Locally, this hump-backed structure has earned the stadium the nick-name the 'Yale Whale'.

The sloping aluminium roofing rests on cables

connected on one side to the concrete arch and on the other to the side walls. These are reinforced by buttresses in a further demonstration of the forces at play in the construction. All in all this design was a structural tour de force, as shown by the tension rods which anchor the building to the ground in order to protect it from heavy snow and wind loads. The expressive roof line, the concave and convex lines and the sculptural treatment of concrete served as a model for Kenzo Tange's famous Olympic Halls in Tokyo.

Interview with

HOK Sports Facilities Group

'A sports facility is an essential ingredient of how you develop and complete the city'

1

2

HOK (Hellmuth, Obata + Kassabaum) Sports Facilities Group was established in 1983 by Ron Labinski and others. In 1973, Labinski was head of Kivvett and Myers' sports where he began to assemble a team of young architects interested in sports design. A few years later, Kivvett and Myer was bought by HNTB. In 1983 Labinski and his colleagues decided to break away from HNTB as they wanted to concentrate on sports architecture. Labinski talked the St. Louis-based architectural firm HOK into opening an office specializing in sports architecture in Kansas City, Missouri.

1. Jacob's Field in Cleveland (Ohio), 1994

2. United Center in Chicago (Illinois)

Can you discuss the relationship between the stadium and the city?
Earl Santee (senior vice president): HOK are all strong urban designers. We believe that the best location for sports venues is in and around the downtown. They are the social centres of the city, the places where people go for leisure or entertainment. It is the best location because it utilizes all the existing resources that the city has to offer. You can actually do a better building because you have context. In the suburbs you can pretty much do whatever you want to do. The building can have any form, shape or idea. In the city you have tremendous context: how it might link to other major events, facilities or venues; how it might relate to parking, to the overall downtown grid and how it may look visually in the city. Stadia have a very significant impact on the city. In a lot of ways they can complete a city downtown. They could be one of the essential ingredients of how you develop a downtown area, whether it is an arena or a stadium with other office functions, with retail and entertainment. So even when people only work from Monday to Friday downtown, they will also come on

Saturdays and Sundays for other reasons which will activate the city on week nights.

Has this development changed the design of the stadium?

In some ways. Generally HOK has been known to design very nostalgic, retro looking baseball parks. At the same time we've been known to design fairly contemporary football or soccer stadia. It depends on the location and the expectations of the client. All sports are different and they want to be different and unique also in their buildings. From an architectural standpoint I don't think that the context of the city should necessarily result in a brick and stone veneer building, it could be concrete, glass, steel, or maybe some new materials that aren't out there yet. Also I think a city shouldn't really have one style. A downtown area should be a collection of different styles which makes it interesting. You have old buildings which are 200 or 300 years old and you have new buildings. The design of a stadium shouldn't necessarily state a certain period of time. It should relate to and fit the overall city.

What about these nostalgic ballparks?

For baseball parks we've been known to design nostalgic venues. It is a ballpark that is downtown, that has arches, brick and stone like granite. Generally they are related to architecture that was known from the late 1800s to the mid-1950s. We would use different materials to fit the city or the organization of massing would be different depending

ball. Even the ballparks that aren't classically styled are still perceived as being nostalgic-looking facilities. Jacob's Field is such an example. It has a steel and glass structure, but with a skin of granite and limestone.

What are the current or future changes in these facilities?

Right now the big issue is that the major sporting teams have decided to brand themselves differently. Since the 1940s football and baseball have shared multi-use facilities. Now almost every major league baseball or NFL team is designing or has designed a specific purpose facility. Multi-use is a different word for mixed use. Mixed use is talking about the different uses like a drug store or a bank within the building that the community can use. I think you will see this more, especially in the more urban sites around the country. There is a transition from multiple use to mixed use.

We always used to think that these facilities were catalysts for development around them and in some cases, like in Denver, that is true. In most cases however it is not, as it has been more a catalyst for re-development: taking the existing infrastructure, warehouses and offices and converting or adapting them to the re-use of the building that relates to the sporting event. I think sport is becoming such an important part of our everyday life, that I can see people living either close by or in the midst of these events.

I think that there is a struggle in the United States: in some ways people want more technologically advanced facilities,

3   4   5

on its placement in the city. We have always used steel as a way to make people feel nostalgic about baseball, as baseball is one of the oldest sports and we wanted to have people relish the days of the 1920s as part of their experience of going to a baseball game.

We have also done a great job in building stadia in different communities, of devising facilities that created a lot of revenue. While some of them were nostalgic, they have become very strong architectural components at the same time. The NFL-stadium in Baltimore has brick on it, but is a very strong piece of architecture that relates to the city on a 365-days-a-year basis. As we move on with other football stadia I think they will have very different looks though. Football generally has not relished its history as much as baseball, so the importance of the architecture from a nostalgic standpoint isn't as important in foot-

3. Hong Kong Stadium, 1994

4. PSI Net Stadium in Baltimore (Maryland), 1998

5. Pepsi Center in Denver (Colorado)

6. Arrowhead Pond in Anaheim (California), 1993

but still, it is all about the sport on the field. For example we've talked about putting video screens in arm chairs for ten years. In San Diego they did it a couple of years ago as they wanted to see how it was going to be used. For years our clients have said: we want to be able to retrofit our seats so we can add those screens. But again I think the people pay more attention to what is on the field or ice, than on their seat. Monitored seats perhaps will be a trend in twenty years, however it is not current. I do think that the seats and the experience will become more personal to the people. Right now people are going to sports events because it is a place where you meet friends. In a lot of ways stadia will become more personal in the way they organize the seating. The facilities will become more in tune with people's preferences, with what they like to eat and do.

Also each seat could be personalized in terms of comfort.

How will these developments affect the look of a stadium?
You will see that many cities will have many different size
venues for each sport. Mid-size arenas for smaller cities
with 10,000 to 12,000 seats will have a growth potential
both in the States and overseas.

    The architecture of the buildings is going to be more
important. It used to be all about seats, but now I think the
expectations of the community and society is that they really
want great architecture. They want to have timeless architecture, they want to be proud of it and relate to it. So each
building has to be better in the way that the architecture
responds to the city. But also how it responds nationally, as
it is really the signature of a city and makes it special versus
other cities.

6

3

The favourite stadium of... *Frits Barend*

sports journalist

'The most beautiful kind of stadium is dying out. Before football had evolved from a sport into a form of entertainment centred on television, stadia were built to play football. The most beautiful stadium that I have known is De Meer, the former stadium of Amsterdam's Ajax football club, which has sadly been demolished. It was never used as a pop concert venue or, even worse, for youth days organized by the Evangelical Broadcasting Company. No matter what the weather or season, the turf was maintained in perfect condition, a pitch exactly as it was meant to be. It was no accident that this was the home turf that produced two of the best soccer players the Netherlands has ever known. I would even dare say that there is some kind of bond between De Meer and the soccer stars Johan Cruijff and Marco van Basten. De Meer was also the birthplace of Piet Keizer's pincer movement. A more masterful yet simple dummy move has never been seen, though it has often been imitated. In De Meer you could hear the players yelling and shouting with joy; you could see the expressions on their faces without the help of a video screen. In De Meer there was also still a real warm-up. If you wanted to have a seat, you had to arrive early. Otherwise you ended up standing high up in the corner of the stands. On the terraces, if you arrived late you were relegated to standing room behind a giant of a man, and later, after the appearance of the first hooligans, to the bottom step behind a fence of barbed wire. But by then De Meer had already lost part of its charm. The warm-up I am talking about is the hour-long wait, guessing who will be in the line-up of players. And then, after yet another verse of a football anthem, the away team would jog onto the pitch. But we weren't interested in them; we were waiting for the red-and-white strip to appear, the home team. You could see them waiting in the narrow tunnel under the grandstand, and if you were sitting close by you could hear the clatter of their boot studs on the tiles and concrete in the tunnel. And then it was that magical moment, a moment without Queen hits, without a hysterical speaker, there was just the accompaniment of civilized applause from the grandstand and polite cheers from the then still uncovered terraces. The players came onto the pitch in style, led by someone like the striker of all strikers Piet Keizer, and lined up on the centre circle with the keeper in the middle, right on the centre spot. Then the toss. If Ajax won, we would play the first half towards the Diemen end; if the opposition won the toss and was quick-witted enough, then Ajax would have to play

towards the city end. After half-time, we would await the arrival of the flocks of seagulls, which usually appeared above the stadium twenty minutes before full time, if there was a gentle southwesterly. They would feast on the churned-up turf as soon as the final whistle was blown. The sound system may have been useless, but that wasn't why you came.

But that's history. Stadia are multifunctional nowadays. Fortunately, De Kuip has been renovated, and has taken over from De Meer. But that is also because of Coentje and De Kromme. I once sat high in the stands at Nou Camp. It was chilly. All you could see was the silhouettes of the players. Perhaps I should make a trip to the modernized Old Trafford. Apparently this is also a stadium purely dedicated to the game of football. Sadly, people watch the match while

eating dinner behind glass in the restaurant here as well.'

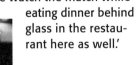

Interview with Dominique Perrault

'How can we build empty space?'

1   2   3   4

Dominique Perrault set up his agency in Paris in 1981. In 1989 he won the international competition for the François Mitterand Bibliothèque de France in Paris, followed by the international competition for the Olympic swimming pool and Velodrome in Berlin in 1992.

1-2. Velodrome and Olympic swimming pool in Berlin, 1997

3. Design for a stadium in Melun-Sénart, 1993

4. Montigala Sports Complex in Badalona, 1998

How would you describe the relationship between large facilities like stadia and the urban fabric?
In the case of the Velodrome in Berlin the programme focused on the city, on the urban fabric. The question was how we could organize a very big volume in this area in former East Berlin, which was completely destroyed. You had these typical Berlin blocks, some terrible high housing buildings and some other parts with old factories. A very special but difficult place. The idea was to build facilities that could help this district grow up and to find an agreeable solution for the people living in the direct surroundings.

I wanted to build a landscape, so I didn't consider the project as a building. When you approach the complex you will only see an orchard with apple trees. The building has disappeared and you will only discover a very flat roof like a lake or a pool. The space has become free and for me it is very important that people can use this space. Organizing only events is not a solution. These different events should be supported by space and the most interesting space in the city is the landscape.

It is also an answer to the existing sport facilities in Berlin. The Velodrome is located on the eastern side of Berlin, on the western side is the old Olympic Stadium, a building with a enormous political and ideological meaning. The Velodrome is an answer to the demonstration of power of the Olympic Stadium: it is in everything the exact opposite.

Most of the stadia are build outside of the city but it would be very interesting if we could develop them in the centre of the city. It is possible to organize, to connect and to develop relationships between a stadium and the city.

It is absolutely sure that we will develop ever bigger programmes, as a result of globalization. It is necessary to combine supermarkets, schools, stadia and factories all together. And that results in a landscape, not in a building. If you imagine these facilities in different buildings next to each other it is terrible. But if you imagine them as part of a landscape, it will be possible to mix them with the city.

What is the difference between this stadium and other stadia?
The Velodrome is not a stadium like a football stadium. Its use is more complex. The swimming pool and the Velodrome are Olympic, but a diversity of other people will use them as well. There are in fact two levels of use of both facilities, one Olympic and one public. In one year you have only 122 days of professional training, while this facility is used every day. Inside they built a special environment for concerts and a lot of other events. This sport complex is like a small city where you can do sports as well as go for a swim or go to a concert and so on. So there are a lot of different facilities and possibilities.

Is a stadium an autonomous design or is it connected to its surroundings?
For me the programme of the building isn't interesting. The question is about emptiness. How can we build empty space in a city? A square, an avenue or a road are empty spaces. How can we create public space for everybody with these kind of big programmes?

I tried to solve this question in a competition which was held for a stadium in the south of Paris, for a new town called Melun-Sénart. My winning design was a landscape. The main idea was to design a big square, with sides of one kilometre. In this square there was a stadium, a training hall, a huge car park (12,000), and an intersection of the high-way and the main road through the new city. The idea was to develop a design with parallel lines of trees with the car park underneath. On these grounds there would be a hill, which was actually the stadium. After an event 80,000 people would walk down the hill to get out of the stadium. It would look like a volcano. The training hall on the other hand was sunken in the field. Neither stadia would be recognizable as such, because they disappeared in the landscape. Hotels, houses, offices and commer-cial buildings would be located around the square. They would function almost as a fence around the space. The space however served as the

main entrance to the city, as people would drive from the highway to the car park underneath and then enter the park.

How will the stadium evolve in the future?
People said about the Velodrome that it was too small. It had only 10,000 seats and to organize big concerts you needed at least 15,000 or 16,000 seats. Perhaps. In fact the size is very comfortable, it is very sweet. Now they show a lot of interest for this medium-sized room, because it is possible to have a political meeting, to present a car, to organize a big party or to invite a philharmonic orchestra. It is possible to organize events which are not very big, but medium-sized. I think it is interesting because it gives new possibilities. In Paris for example we have some huge con-ference halls, and some very, very big places for sport, but in between there is nothing.

Part of city

Stadio Luigi Ferraris

name: Stadio Luigi Ferraris
place: Genoa, Italy
date of construction: 1987-1989
architects: Gregotti Associati, A. Cagnardi,
P. Cerri, V. Gregotti
capacity: 44,600

Wedged between a river to the south, a prison to the west, housing to the east and a four-teenth-century villa to the north, stands the striking Luigi Ferraris stadium. In the midst of a lively working-class district, the four 'Pompeian red' towers from which are suspended the steel girders supporting the rectilinear roof sections, are compelling eye-catchers. The towers are the inner-urban version of the light masts that signal the presence of a sports ground all around the world. They sit atop the four similarly coloured corner blocks which contain the ramps leading to the second tier of seats. From the outside, the light concrete ramps are visible as a zebra-crossing through a large opening in the side wall.

Gregotti's design replaced the old Stadio Luigi Ferraris, built on this site in 1928. The old stadium had undergone frequent partial renovations over the years but with the 1990 World Cup in prospect it was finally judged too outdated for mere refurbishment and it was decided to build a brand new stadium. The location in the middle of the city brought with it a whole range a problems: the site was tight, the building height was restricted on account of the surrounding apartment blocks and the supply and removal of building materials was difficult. What is more, the Genoa and Samdoria football clubs had to be able to continue using the ground during construction. For this reason, the builders began by demolishing and replacing the southern half of the old stadium. Only then did work commence on the other half. The stadium has consequently never looked entirely new: by the time the stadium was completed, the walls of the southern half were covered with graffiti, just like old times.

Oriole Baseball Park Camden Yards

name: Oriole Baseball Park Camden Yards
place: Baltimore, United States
date of construction: 1992
architect: HOK Sports Facilities Group
capacity: 48,188

In the United States it has been customary for big multi-purpose stadia to be built on the outskirts of cities. With the opening in 1992 of the Oriole Baseball Park in the middle of the run-down inner-city area of Baltimore, it became clear that a stadium can also be an agent of urban regeneration. HOK's design takes its cue from the existing surroundings and from the baseball stadia of the 1930s and 1940s.

The huge V-shaped stand consists of three decks and is faced in traditional brick on the outside. The pitch is sunken so that the circulation gallery providing access to the stands is at street level. The stands themselves contain various spectator facilities plus 72 hospitality boxes and three reception rooms.

The design incorporates an old warehouse (1898) which serves as a backdrop to right field and lends the stadium a historical aura. The warehouse contains shops, pubs, restaurants and a museum and is separated from the stadium by an eleven-metre-wide promenade, the continuation of Eutaw Street, the thoroughfare linking the stadium with the city centre.

Camden Yards has helped to revive the dilapidated inner-city area and to strengthen urban functions. Many American cities have followed Baltimore's example and are trying to combat inner-urban degeneration by building a stadium or big sports centre. In the process, sporting facilities are returning to the place where they belong, in the middle of the community.

Stade de France

name: Stade de France
place: Paris, France
date of construction: 1995-1998
architects: M. Macary, A. Zubléna,
M. Regembal, C. Constantini
capacity: 80,000

Built for the final round of the last World Cup of the twentieth century, the Stade de France represented the official canonization of football. Here the ultimate high mass (World Cup Final) was celebrated by 80,000 faithful beneath a roof that floated like a gigantic halo above the zone of the gods. Television delivered the host directly into the living rooms of a further 4 billion or so communicants.

The stadium was built on a derelict industrial site, wedged between a canal, a railway line and the Boulevard Périphérique, close to one of the busiest traffic interchanges around Paris. It was intended to initiate the redevelopment of Saint-Denis.

The stadium is elliptical in plan and consists of three rings of stands, the lowest of which can be moved backwards and forwards on air cushions. For soccer and rugby matches it is moved close in to the pitch; when retracted it reveals an athletics track.

On the outside the stadium is clad in a net of stainless steel mesh which lends a sense of unity to this complex stadium machine: in addition to sporting facilities, press rooms and restaurants, Stade de France contains a conference and exhibition centre, 4,000 m² retail space and 2,000 m² office space underneath the stands.

The visual appearance of the stadium is dictated by the gigantic dimensions of the oval roof that is suspended from eighteen 60-metre-high poles. At night, when it is lit from below, a radiant aureole floats above the cathedral of Saint-Denis.

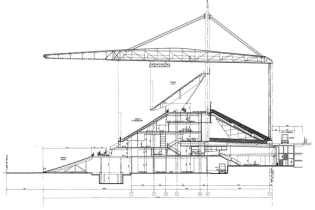

Stadion Feyenoord

name: Stadion Feyenoord (De Kuip)
place: Rotterdam, the Netherlands
date of construction: 1934-1936
architects: J.A. Brinkman & L.C. van der Vlugt
capacity: 65,000
renovation: 1994
architects: Architectenbureau Van den Broek & Bakema and
Zwarts & Jansma Architecten
capacity: 52,000

'Big-headed' was how the newspapers in 1934 described Feyenoord's plans to build a stadium for 60,000 to 70,000 spectators. A few years earlier the Olympic Stadium seating only 32,000 spectators, had been built in Amsterdam at a cost of over five million guilders. Now the world was in the grip of an economic depression and the Rotterdam football club had only 600 members, some of whom were out of work.

The club management threw in their lot with Brinkman & Van der Vlugt, the architectural practice that had just won international recognition with their design for the Van Nelle factory. Taking the two-tier West Stand at London's Highbury Park as their model, the architects designed a stadium

encircled by two tiers of stands. Unlike in London, the second tier did not need to be supported on columns which greatly improved the spectators' view of the pitch. This revolutionary design became a model for many internationally famous stadia, such as Nou Camp and Bernabeu in Spain and San Siro in Milan

The use of modern materials and the functionalist design (a fine-meshed steel frame supporting the concrete stands, designed to harmonize with the dockland setting) make the

stadium one of the high points of Dutch Functionalism. Despite its size, the oval stadium gives an impression of intimacy because all the spectators are close to the pitch.

In 1994 the stadium underwent extensive refurbishment. It acquired a new, wrap-around roof. An annexe containing offices, business facilities and a restaurant was placed in front of the stadium on the east side and the seats of honour were moved to this side. Escalators link the annexe with the stadium. Blue bucket seats replaced the old terraces.

Thanks to this renovation the Feyenoord stadium now satisfies all the FIFA and EUFA requirements with the result that it has been chosen to host the final of Euro 2000.

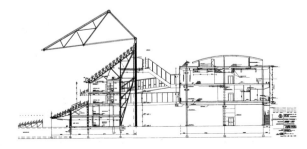

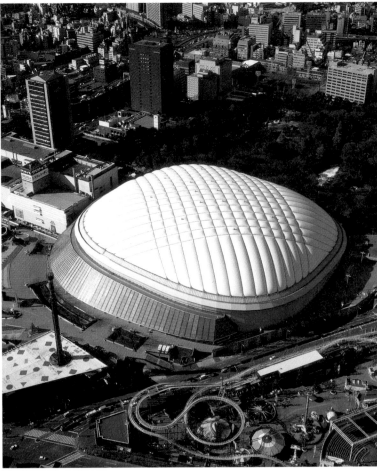

Tokyo Dome

name: Tokyo Dome
place: Tokyo, Japan
date of construction: 1985-1988
architects: Korakuen Air Dome Joint Design
Team: Nikken Sekkei and Takenaka
Corporation
capacity: 55,000

The Tokyo Dome, the first covered stadium in Japan, is used mainly for baseball, a sport that is very popular with the Japanese. The Dome is home to two Major League teams, the all powerful Yomiuri Giants and the lower placed Fighters. It is also frequently used for conventions and pop concerts. In fact the stadium is least suited to sporting events, and players and fans complain bitterly about the fact that balls hit into the outfield can barely be distinguished from the white underside of the roof.

The stadium is square in plan with rounded corners, but the stands follow the layout of American baseball stadia: behind home plate there are three tiers of seats and behind the outfield one. In addition, there are luxury suites on the first balcony. The stadium owes is nickname 'the Big Egg' to the roof which is made of teflon-coated fibreglass stretched between cables. This limp membrane structure is held aloft by air pressure which is 0.3 per cent higher inside the dome than outside.

The most important aspect of the Tokyo Dome design is the creation of a large entertainment zone around the stadium, with bowling alleys, a roller skating rink, slot machine halls, a sauna, a hotel, theatres, sporting facilities, a swimming pool, shops, a baseball museum and amusement parks. The complex is served by a railway station and two metro stations. The embedding of the sports facility in an entertainment zone guarantees the visitor a complete day out.

Tokyo Metropolitan Gymnasium

name: Tokyo Metropolitan Gymnasium
place: Tokyo, Japan
date of construction: 1984-1990
architect: Fumihiko Maki
capacity: 10,000

Like Kenzo Tange's Olympic arena, this sporting complex by Fumihiko Maki is set in a spacious urban park; they stand not far from one another in the middle of the city. Maki's design comprises four sporting facilities: a big sports arena for 10,000 spectators, a smaller one for 2,300 spectators, an indoor pool with 900 seats and an open-air athletics track.

Of the three, clearly differentiated buildings, the large sports arena is the most striking. Its expressive roof curves over the circular building like a mussel shell. It is supported on two steel arches and consists of an ingenious construction of steel girders, a 'floating' structure borrowed from Tange's Olympic Hall. The smaller sports arena is a simple, orthogonal structure topped by a pyramidal roof. The similarly rectangular swimming pool has a neutral, almost flat roof.

The archetypical roofs, all of the same material, define the complex's appearance. This effect is reinforced by the fact that the buildings have been dug into the ground. The layout of the outdoor space exploits the resulting differences in height. The forecourt of the large building is an artificial valley linked by steps to the remaining public space.

And herein lies the essential difference between the two sports complexes. Where Tange's centre stands in solitary splendour in an isolated park, Maki has integrated the sports park with the city. The loose composition of individually designed elements is held together by the intervening public spaces which are directly related to the city. The whole reflects the complexity of the surrounding urban fabric and is emphatically part of urban life; the area is used day and night.

Body and emotion

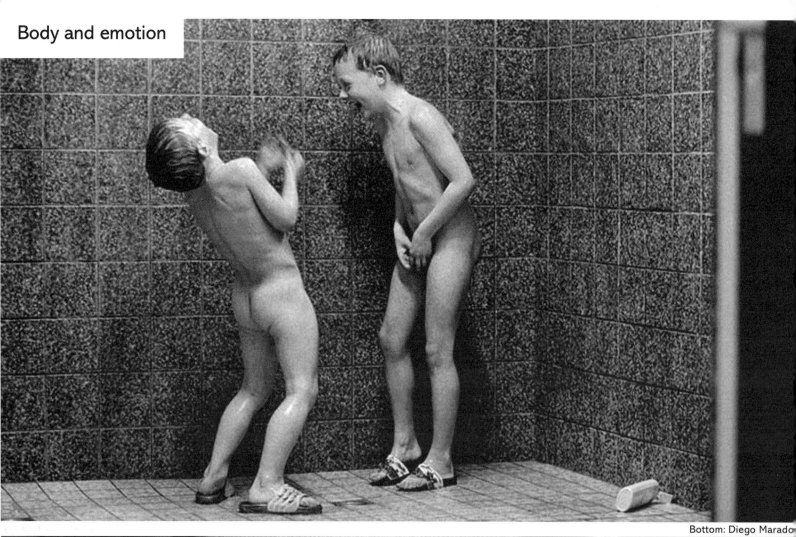

Bottom: Diego Marado

top: Ronald Ophuis, Voetballers II (Soccer players), 1996

: Martijn Reuser

bottom: Dennis Bergkamp

The last twenty years have seen a real boom in the construction of stadia in the United States, Asia and Europe. Stadia are being built one after the other, equipped with all manner of technical innovations and often accompanied by the construction of new hotels, restaurants, and other facilities. These stadia are part of the large-scale building projects that many cities have instigated in order to improve their profile and sharpen their image. Now that cities are no longer automatically the place for collective facilities to be located, establishing these profiles has become a major concern. The combination of increasing mobility and the recent emergence of modern technologies has seriously undermined the traditional significance of the city. And this applies more emphatically in the United States – where many cities do not have an historic centre – than in Europe. In contrast with the decades immediately after the Second World War, planners in the United States are striving to arrest the migration to the peripheries of the cities, and the corresponding demise of downtown areas, by constructing shopping malls, festival markets, museums, amusement parks and stadia. Just like the shopping malls which have proven their usefulness in improving the competitive position of a city, stadia are also being used as part of the weaponry in the battle of the cities.

Stadium fever

The pride and presence of a professional football team is more important than 30 libraries.[1]
(Art Modell, owner of the Cleveland Browns baseball team)

Marieke van Rooij

Early Days

Football, or soccer, was born on the pastures green of the English universities and public schools in the late nineteenth century. Initially played by an elite, football soon became more widespread, but it was not until the working classes discovered the game that it made a really big breakthrough. Factory directors encouraged this, founding clubs and establishing football pitches close to the factories, because they realized that soccer would keep their employees in better condition than hanging around down the pub. These fields were located in the least desirable land on the edges of towns, which a larger public could only reach when the public transport system was established, making it possible for the working class to travel to the football grounds. In the pre-automobile era, the situation of football grounds close to railway stations made them more easily accessible for the supporters of away teams. The stadia, which were still closely linked with the important industrial giants, stayed put while the towns and cities expanded around them, and were eventually surrounded by residential suburbs. 'These grounds had been built for a generation of fans that didn't drive, or even rely on public transport overly much, and so they were placed carefully in the middle of residential areas full of narrow streets and terraced houses. Twenty or thirty years after the catchment areas began to expand dramatically, and people started travelling from ten or twenty or fifty miles away, nothing has changed. This was the time to build new stadia, out of town, with parking facilities and improved safety provisions; the rest of Europe did, and as a consequence the grounds in Italy, Spain, Portugal and France are bigger, better and safer, but typically, in a country whose infrastructure is finally beginning to fall apart, we didn't bother. Here, tens of thousands of fans walk up narrow, winding underground tunnels, or double-park their cars in tiny, quiet, local streets, while the relevant football authorities seem content to carry on as if nothing at all – behaviour, the fan base, methods of transport, even the state of the ground themselves, which like the rest of us start to look a bit tatty after the first half-century or so – had changed. There was so much that could and should have been done, and nothing ever was, and everyone trundled along for year after year, for a hundred years, until Hillsborough.'[2]

It was only in the wake of tragic accidents at the old British stadia (Bolton

Side entrance to Arsenal's Highbury Stadium in London

1946, Ibrox 1971, Hillsborough 1989) that new stadia have been constructed there. The British clubs, however, seem to find it very difficult to abandon their old homes. An example of a club like this is Arsenal, which plays at the magnificent old Highbury, in the midst of a densely populated London borough. The stadium's inconspicuous entrances stand amidst rows of houses, the little gardens of which back up to the blank walls behind the stands. Over the years the club has replaced the stands, but Arsenal's continuing unprecedented popularity means that the club actually needs a larger stadium with modern facilities and, most especially, more parking space. A new stadium has been on the cards for a long time, but the club has not managed to cut the Gordian knot. One reason for this is the fear that they will lose the support of devoted fans. In his book Fever Pitch, Nick Hornby describes his experiences with Arsenal football club: 'Every time a club mentions a new stadium, there is an outcry; when Arsenal and Tottenham mooted ground-sharing a few years back, at a projected site near, I think, Alexandra Palace, the protests were loud and long ('Tradition!'),

and as a consequence we now find ourselves with an assortment of the tiniest stadia in the world.'[3]

Following the example of the British industrial giants, private companies in continental Europe also established football clubs: Italian car manufacturers FIAT founded Juventus, and Dutch electronics giant Philips founded PSV. In sharp contrast with the situation in Britain, municipal authorities on the continent readily accepted civic responsibility for the construction of many of these stadia. This was partly because different social and political attitudes prevailed on the continent, and partly because the municipalities realized that it would lend their town or city a prestigious status. The municipal stadia in continental Europe were not used for football alone, as in Britain; but were based on the Olympic model, and thus suitable for various sports. This meant that many of the stadia had an athletics track around the football pitch, and the spectators were therefore further away from the game. Different clubs often used the same stadium as well.[4] This also reduced a stadium's intimacy.

Major League competition

In the United States baseball was the most popular sport. Baseball fields were set up on the cheap land just outside the city centres because industrialization had already devoured all the vacant areas in the city centres, as in Europe. Baseball also started out as a sport for the elite: workers could not afford to travel to the baseball fields and, moreover, the games were played when ordinary folk had to work. In the 1920s, when ticket prices dropped and the games were played on Sundays or in the evenings, baseball did become extremely popular. Wealthy industrialists discovered the sport and saw the construction of a stadium as a safe investment. These private individuals or businesses developed most of the stadia constructed in the 1920s and 1930s. Although there were only a few municipalities which invested in stadia, these facilities were still enjoyed as civic status symbols. 'In an urban area aspiring to first-class status, a major league team playing in a large modern stadium was as vital as a symphony or an art museum.'[5]

These pre-war stadia were in need of modernization by the 1950s, but the owners opted for the construction of completely new stadia instead of renovation. Bigger and more comfortable stadia followed in the wake of the suburbanization of city outskirts, where land was cheap and the stadium would be easily accessible by car. There was such a massive exodus from the American city centres at this time that suburbanites considered it dangerous to visit the old stadia downtown. The historic Comiskey Park in Chicago almost had to close its doors because of pressure from supporters who no longer dared to go downtown.[6]

The increase in automobility not only determined the location of the stadia, but also demanded special infrastructural planning. People no longer used public transport to get to the stadia; the vast majority came by car. The stadium became a self-sufficient object surrounded by a sea of asphalt, estranged from its surroundings.

Local and provincial governments were subjected to increasing pressure to help defray the costs of these new stadia. The financing of these large multifunctional projects was now beyond the independent means of the private owners. What is more, these entrepreneurial owners were all too aware of the perceived importance of a large stadium for a city, and they took full advantage of this trump card in negotiations

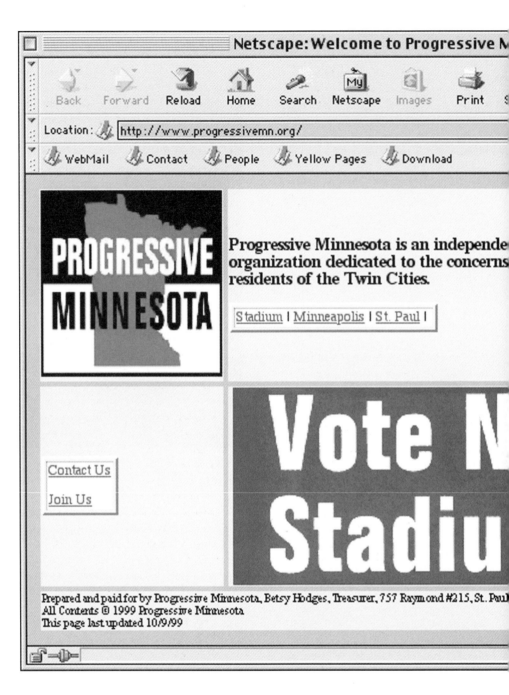

with the civic or governmental authorities.

The prestige factor began to play a big role. Cities discovered that they could attract a Major League team by building a well-equipped, modern stadium. The first city in the United States to use this strategy was Milwaukee. And they succeeded, because the owner of the Boston Braves decided to move his team to Milwaukee. During the first seasons they attracted six times as many fans as they had in Boston. When the club's success dwindled, however, the Braves sought their salvation in Atlanta. After 13 seasons, Milwaukee once again had to attract a replacement for the Braves, a team they had

recruited not so long ago. But this time they only had an outdated stadium in hand.

The example set by Milwaukee in 1953 marked the start of the mass migration of sports teams that still continues today. Cities that do not have a Major League team in residence construct a new stadium in order to attract one, while cities that are already host to a Major League team build a new stadium in order to prevent them leaving. There is always a reason to build a bigger, better, more innovative stadium.

What are the reasons for these cities imposing special taxes in order to subsidize the

The threat of their going elsewhere always played a role in the background. This is quite unlike the situation in Europe, where the clubs are traditionally much more closely tied to a particular city. It is unthinkable that the soccer club Feyenoord would move from Rotterdam to Amsterdam, simply because Amsterdam offered the club a more beautiful stadium.

A second reason for the construction of a new stadium is the conviction that it is a sound investment. Its presence would create new jobs for the residents of neighbouring communities, directly associated with the stadium or with spin-off commercial activities that established themselves close by. In reality, the number of new jobs often fails to offset the investment by local or national government. Research by the economist Robert A. Baade has shown that the 30 stadia recently constructed for 27 municipalities had not resulted in additional income or jobs.[8] All that it achieved was a shift in income from one part of the amusement sector to another. Opponents argue that all the money spent on building stadia could better be directed towards better education and social services. Two representatives of these opposition groups, Joanna Cagan and Neil deMause, compare the situation outlined above with the way in which the western world invests in the developing world: 'In some ways, the public funding of huge stadium projects, outdoor malls, and casino halls, coupled with enormous cuts in local spending on social services, can almost be viewed as the domestic version of the structural adjustment plans pushed on developing nations (and increasingly Western Europe as well) by the World Bank and the International Monetary Fund. The formula is simple: Devote ever-decreasing amounts of public wealth to support the services needed by the poor and helpless, and invest more and more in ways that will return increasing profits to the small numbers of rich and privileged.'[9] Despite the many reports that have repeatedly indicate that investment in stadia is a loss- rather than a profit-maker, and despite the many activist groups that are calling for the preservation of old stadia and protesting the construction of new stadia, deMause and Cagan claim that cities in the United States spent a total of about $750 million on the construction or renovation of stadia between 1980 and 1990, and the total for the 1990s will amount to between $8 and $11 billion.[10]

The stadium accommodations in Minneapolis and St. Paul, the Twin Cities, are notable examples of the developments outlined above. The government-subsidized Metropolitan Stadium ('Met') was the first stadium from the 1950s to be replaced by the multifunctional Metrodome in 1982. The director of the Vikings Football club had asked for a new stadium because he thought the Met was too small and too cold. He wanted a covered stadium. That was pretty surprising considering there were only a few clubs in the United States who played in a covered stadium at that time (1973). The director argued that his proposal was not in his own interests, but rather those of the city: 'The Vikings would play in any other facility in the metropolitan area, including the University of Minnesota's Memorial Stadium, but they preferred a new stadium in downtown Minneapolis or St. Paul to benefit the city's downtown area.'[11] The city imposed a new tax on hotel and motel rooms and alcohol, and constructed a new stadium.

The Metrodome is part of a comprehensive leisure complex, as are many other American stadia. The stadium is surrounded by a 'Hall of Fame', restaurants and discotheques. Going to a sports event has become a whole day out. An additional attraction is an open space where people can set up their barbecues, play interactive games, or listen to a live band booked by the teams, and where there are permanent sanitary facilities.[12]

Even this hyper-modern stadium did not completely satisfy the Twin Cities' sports teams. Last year, the Minnesota Twins lobbied for a new baseball stadium to be built by Ellerbe Becket. But this time city residents voted against the use of municipal funds to pay for the stadium's construction in a referendum. Two action groups were formed to scuttle the deal. Their web site states: 'Our goal is to educate the citizens of St. Paul on the financial realities surrounding the issue of whether to vote to raise the sales tax rate in the city by nearly nine million dollars per year to finance a new stadium for the Minnesota Twins.'[13] On the web site Field of Schemes produced by Joanna Cagan and Neil deMause, underlines the absurdity of the battle for the construction of stadia. Topping the list of the ten most far-fetched reasons to build a stadium is the following: 'IT'S THE CURE FOR CANCER. In the weeks before a legislative vote on a new stadium, the Minnesota Twins ran a TV commercial featuring a ballplayer visiting a boy in a hospital. A voiceover announced, "If the Twins

construction of stadia? The main reason is prestige: without a Major League team and the stadium to match it, a city simply does not count. Michael Danielson, who has made an excellent and detailed study of the commercial aspects of sport, wrote: 'Art museums, symphony orchestras, theaters, and zoos are all marks of major cities, as are libraries and universities, leading law firms and banks, and great commercial and industrial corporations, but big league teams are seen by many as more easily and widely recognized symbols of a place's importance.'[7] Team owners are more than happy to exploit a city's fear of losing face in pursuit of their extravagant demands.

leave Minnesota, an 8-year old from Willmar undergoing chemotherapy will never get a visit from Marty Cordova." It later turned out that the boy had already died by the time the commercial aired.'14

From multifunctionality to the creation of a commercial district

At the start of the twentieth century, stadia were constructed purely for the practice and watching of sport. The facilities were limited to an informal hotdog stand and the place to meet people was the bar on the corner. After the Second World War, people realized that the size and flexibility of a stadium, and the crowds that it attracted, made it suitable for all kinds of other activities. The stadium was transformed from a temple of sport into a multifunctional corporation. This caught on much faster in the United States than in Europe, and America still leads the way.

The Astrodome in Houston (1965) was an innovative stadium project. As well as providing accommodation for different sports (baseball, American football, athletics) it could also host a whole range of events. This was possible because the Astrodome was completely covered. It was also the first stadium in the United States with skyboxes, glass boxes with luxurious seats that were sold for a hefty premium to the privileged big-spenders. In the 1960s and 1970s, this kind of multifunctional stadium, suitable for a variety of sports, became the norm in the United States.

It took a while before this trend reached Europe. One of the first European experiments with this kind of stadium was the Galgenwaard stadium (1977-1982) in Utrecht, built by Ballast Nedam/Etten/Zinsmeister. The stadium looks like a run-of-the-mill office building from the outside and provides accommodation for companies, with a view of the pitch. Although it is not the most elegant stadium in the world, it works surprisingly well. Numerous delegations from the Netherlands and abroad have visited Galgenwaard in order to see how it functions. The management is now planning a refurbishment and substantial expansion of the stadium, increasing capacity from 14,000 to 25,000 spectators. The stadium will continue to be multifunctional, but the characteristic tympanum occupied by the companies will probably be dropped.

The Louis II stadium (1985) for 20,000 spectators in Monaco, designed by Henri Pottier, takes the notion of multifunctionality much further. It was necessary to construct it

in the middle of the city, because Monaco simply has so little space available. Because of this prominent location, the exterior of the stadium was subject to strict programmatic requirements: each façade had to blend in with the surrounding buildings. And this did not only result in an exterior with such a unique form; the interior is spectacular too. The playing field is raised, standing at about

the height of the third stories of the surrounding buildings. Underneath it there is a car park (1,750 parking places), a swimming pool (500 spectators), and a sports hall (2,200 -3,500 spectators). The stadium expert Simon Inglis described his impressions on entering the Louis II stadium: 'Yet the first thing which confounds most visitors, as they arrive at the stadium's main entrance, is that there should be a football ground at all behind the façade; it is, apparently, no more than a collection of shops and offices, albeit ranged attractively in blocks of varying heights with modern, post–modern and traditional forms happily commingling.'15

The topper in terms of multi-functionality is the SkyDome in Toronto, Canada, designed by Rod Robbie and inaugurated in 1989. It was built on the site of an old railway sidings and has a capacity for 50,000 spectators. Alongside the sports accommodation there is a restaurant on three floors with a view of the pitch, a Hard Rock Cafe, a multiplex cinema, a shopping centre, a miniature golf course, and a hotel with 346 rooms, including 70 luxury suites with a spectacular view of the playing field. Of course these ringside suites have spawned tales about an amorous couple making love in front of the window, thereby attracting more attention than the players on the pitch.16 The stadium is used for American football and baseball and, because of the sliding roof, can also be used for a whole variety of other events. In 1990, the stadium was booked for activities on 185 days of the

Globe Arena in Stockholm, 1989

year, but even this was not sufficient to repay the debts with which the city had saddled itself in order to finance the stadium; the project had cost a whole CA$578 million, instead of the budgeted CA$150 million.

The SkyDome is not an isolated construction but forms part of an entertainment, shopping and business district, including the massive CN tower. About CA$2 billion was spent on making the area into a real tourist attraction.

Trends in Europe

The recent developments in North America can hardly be compared with the general trend in Europe, where there is still very little evidence of the combination of sport and commerce. The stadium is still rarely considered as part of a complete 'entertainment factory', but stadia are occasionally being designed to form the core of a commercial district, particularly in northern and central Europe.

The Ice Hockey Dome in Stockholm, with its eye-catching design, is an early example. This dome, constructed by Berg Arkitektkontor AB for the 1989 World Championships, stands at the heart of a shopping centre, offices, hotels and residential units that cover a total area of about 130,000 m². This combination of functions was the result of a collaboration between the city and private investors. The collaboration between these two groups was essential to the success of a whole new district like this. Public-private funding is becoming increasingly popular in Europe, where until recently the financing of stadia was principally a burden for municipal authorities. Europe has thus ended up following in the footsteps of the United States, but it has arrived at this form of public-private collaboration from a completely different direction.

The location of the Amsterdam ArenA is similar to that of the Ice Hockey Dome in Stockholm. The ArenA (1993-1996), designed by Schuurman and Soeters, is set in an area that was primarily a business district. The construction of the stadium has transformed the character and function of the district, turning it into a varied urban environment that will provide space for offices, shops and entertainment. The ArenA forms the centrepiece for an area based on the American model. Henk Markerink, the stadium's managing director, said: 'We travelled all round the world in order to pick up ideas for the ArenA, and we eventually decided on the American Superdome concept. We want to

Location plan Amsterdam ArenA, 1996

recreate the American hospitality principle in a stadium that is comfortable and has every imaginable convenience: a sports event has to be an excuse for a whole day out. We also want to emulate the American commercial approach, with merchandising and sponsoring.'[17] The original plan was to construct the stadium opposite a triangle of leisure facilities, Markerink explained: 'Pathé Cinemas is working on plans for a massive multiplex cinema, Endemol wants to build a new theatre, and Mojo concert organizers is talking about a concert hall. There will also be a shopping centre. All in all, we have set our sights on becoming the Broadway of Amsterdam.'[18]

Sport as entertainment, as part of the American notion of a 'day out' for the whole family, is still the exception rather than the rule in Europe. After Endemol Entertainment withdrew its participation in the leisure triangle opposite the ArenA, it took a long time to find investors. While the stadium is already fully functional, the other facilities, including a cinema, a concert hall and a theatre, are

still either under construction or in the development phase. Out-of-town recreation and leisure complexes in Europe always have to compete with the historic city centres. A spokesman from the department store De Bijenkorf asked: 'Why would people hang around in that environment after a match or a show, when the urban rail system can transport them to the buzzing heart of Amsterdam in just 10 minutes?'[19]

The Stade de France (1995-1998), built to a design by Macaray/Zubléna/Regembal/Constantini, in the Paris suburb of Saint Denis, was also supposed to form part of a mixed commercial-residential district with offices, shops and residential accommodation.[20] The full realization of this plan is still highly uncertain as the construction of parks, gardens and the connections with the surrounding city areas have failed to live up to expectations. The critic Harm Tilman believes that it may now be difficult to find any sound developer who is still prepared to invest in the area. The stadium functions as a status symbol for Paris and St. Denis rather than effecting a real economic regeneration. The St. Denis district council was keen to get in on the 'Grands Projets' along the lines of the Opéra-Bastille, the Bibliothèque Nationale and La Défense in order to rid itself of its image as a poverty-stricken and problematic suburb. During negotiations, the mayor of St. Denis lobbied for the enclosure of a kilometre-long section of the A1 motorway that cuts through St. Denis, the extension of the metro line, and the construction of two new stations. Though all these objectives have been fulfilled, it has not yet led to a regeneration of the immediate surroundings. Visitors to the imposing stadium are confronted with a massive colossus that is enclosed by motorways and a canal, completely isolated from its surroundings. The only economic activity in the immediate surroundings amounts to a miserable building with a Quick fast-food restaurant, a cinema, and a Decathlon sports shop. The deserted, poorly maintained parking areas, and the out-of-work circus that has struck camp on the route to the metro station, only emphasize the sense of desolation. The Stade de France is certainly not the powerhouse of a new urbanism that the stadium's publicists claim in their press package: 'One of the key features in the architecture of the Stade de France is the open view towards the city. In ancient times, amphitheatres were magnificent urban objects. The Stade de France re-establishes a link with this tradition by becoming the driving force of a new urbanism.'[21]

Revitalizing the American downtown

In the United States, where cities have been subject to an ongoing exodus and impoverishment, the city authorities have now introduced active policies to inject new life into the empty centres, using ambitious regeneration programmes. After the 'festival markets' and 'shopping malls' it is now the turn of the stadia to play their part in the effort to arrest and reverse this phenomenon. The conviction of the United States that these regeneration projects are worthwhile is clear from the sum of $16 billion that was invested in entertainment projects between 1989 and 1999.[22] New stadia are no longer being constructed in the suburbs but right in the city centres, surrounded by amusement and recreation facilities. The revitalization is an important reason for the city authorities to finance these projects. Cleveland, Baltimore, Chicago and Detroit are examples of cities

Stade de France in Paris, 1998

that have faced economic difficulties because of de-industrialization, and are striving to prevent the degeneration of the city centres with large-scale entertainment projects. Despite the fact that the stadia attract a great many visitors, the positive impact on the neighbouring districts is questionable. After all, the stadia provide enough commercial activities of their own, and thus usually remain isolated little islands in the inner city.

In 1995, the owner of the Cleveland Browns, Art Modell, announced that his team was moving to Baltimore. This departure shocked Cleveland but was cause for celebration in the city of Baltimore, which had been looking for a replacement for the Baltimore Colts since this team had left for Indianapolis in 1984. After the Colts' emigration, Baltimore had built a new stadium and had tried everything to attract a new team. Modell chose the city of Baltimore because of the extremely attractive conditions that his team was offered. Cleveland then built a new stadium for a franchise the National Football League had promised the city, which was to be decided in 1999. The new stadia were located down-

town and were more intimate than the previous generation of stadia because they were only intended to accommodate one sport.

The urban location demanded a different design, in order to establish a connection with the surroundings. This involved an architectural element that stadia on the city outskirts had usually lacked: a façade. The designs harked back to the familiar nostalgia of the pre-war stadia. Instead of being called stadia, they were called 'ballparks'.

The Oriole Ballpark that is part of Camden Yards in Baltimore, designed by HOK and opened in 1992, marked the start of this type of development. The old restored warehouses on this former industrial terrain form the backdrop for the stadium. Alongside the baseball stadium, Camden Yards also has an American football stadium, and these are the focal points of a completely new district with shops, offices and tourist attractions such as the National Aquarium and Maryland Science Center, to the west of Baltimore's inner harbour. The district is a key element in the development of the coastline.

Oriole Baseball Park in Baltimore, 1992

There are now so many of these nostalgic stadia in the United States that the retro stadium, originally intended as a specific building for a specific location, has already been reduced to a cliché. Designers search out an historical image, then repeat it ad infinitum.

The Gateway Center in Cleveland is very similar to Camden Yards. Instead of being part of a dockside area, the Gateway Center occupies a riverside position on the Cuyahoga. The development also includes two stadia, restaurants, clubs, and no fewer than three museums, namely the Rock & Roll Hall of Fame, the Maritime Museum and the Great Lake Science Center. The Gateway Center was financed by a whole variety of means: loans, donations from the state, licensing fees for the trademarks of both stadia, income from parking fees, income from special 'seats' in the stadia, and revenue from a special tax on alcohol and tobacco products. The city used all this funding to revitalize the 'downtown' area and put it back on the map. It gave Cleveland an opportunity to rid itself of its negative image: 'Cleveland

was better known as the site of the Cuyahoga River which became so polluted with industrial waste that it once caught fire.'[23]

Revitalisation in Europe
The situation in the inner cities of Europe is much less drastic than in the United States. There is no worrying exodus from the historic city centres, and nor is there such an alarmingly high crime rate. Nonetheless, there are

Jacob's Field in Cleveland, 1994

still a few European cities that have opted to construct stadia in their centres, motivated by the need for urban regeneration.

Cardiff in Wales is one example. The choice of an urban location was a surprise even in Britain, because the Taylor Report – published in 1989 in the wake of the Hillsborough tragedy – recommended the construction of new stadia in suburban areas. Nevertheless, the planners decided to locate Cardiff's Millennium Stadium (1999), a rugby stadium designed by HOK+LOBB, on an abandoned industrial zone on the banks of the river in the city centre. This stadium has a sliding roof, just like Amsterdam's ArenA, which means that it can host various events throughout the year. The stadium forms the heart of an area that is expected to give a new lease of life to the whole western side of the city by developing the waterfront (exactly like the examples in the United States mentioned above). In addition it serves to attract tourists to the whole of Wales, and was therefore primarily financed with funds from the Millennium Committee.

A recent example in the Netherlands is the city of Groningen, where plans have been tabled for a state-of-the-art stadium. In recent years, Groningen has been trying to establish an image as the 'Capital of the North' of the Netherlands, and is undergoing a complete metamorphosis. This started with a number of architecture festivals and the construction of a new museum by Alessandro Mendini, to be followed by this new stadium by architect Wiel Arets. It will be a multifunctional stadium, incorporating a whole range of facilities for the city. The remarkable exterior was designed with the underlying idea that the complex will also be a tourist attraction.

During the 1990s, the city of Genoa made every effort to give a positive twist to its image as an industrial city. As in Baltimore, the waterfront has been completely redeveloped for tourism, with one of Europe's largest aquariums and a harbour for leisure craft. Renzo Piano was responsible for the design of this redevelopment. A new stadium, which was needed for the football World Championships in 1990, fitted in perfectly this urban renewal process. As with Monaco, Genoa has a lack of space, and the planners therefore decided to construct the new stadium on the site of the old one (from 1928), integrating part of the old entrance in the new design. Because the stadium stands in an extremely densely populated neighbourhood, surrounded by residential buildings and a prison complex, the developers hoped that the stadium would inject this neighbourhood with a new lease of life. One element that was intended to contribute to this regeneration process was the shop space that architect Vittorio Gregotti introduced beneath the stands. These shops, which are the most dominant feature in the façade, meant that the stadium could actually be integrated in the local street life. However, all except two of these shops are still standing

vacant, which has a sad impact rather than a sense of regeneration.

The Charlety Stadium (1994) in Paris, designed by Henry and Bruno Gaudin, was a project that did not pretend to effect a wider regeneration. Nevertheless, it is extremely well integrated in the urban environment and has afforded the area around the Porte de Gentilly a new identity. The new stadium was built on the site of the demolished stadium (1938) and is situated on the edge of the city, where it is surrounded by a cemetery, the ring road and flats. Because it stands on a hill, it commands a view of the large office buildings around the Place d'Italie, the China Town of Paris. The stadium is part of a

complex with offices, tennis courts, an underground sports hall, and a park. These sports facilities are used by the university sports club. Because of this combination of functions, the stadium has been very successfully integrated in the urban fabric. This has been facilitated by the relatively small size of the stadium, which, with a capacity of 20,000 spectators, is considerably smaller than the Stade de France (80,000 spectators). The stadium, with a strip of parkland to the north, overlooks the cemetery, while the large office complex on the opposite side establishes a link with the residential areas. The view between the various rings, which makes references to the Stadio Communale by Pier

Luigi Ferraris stadium in Genoa, 1990
Vacant retail space beneath the stand of the Luigi Ferraris stadium in Genoa, 1990
Stade de Charlety in Paris, 1994

Stadium fever

133

Luigi Nervi (Florence, 1932) establishes a connection with the surroundings.

The Olympics

Hosting a large-scale sports event is a much more effective way for a city to achieve worldwide fame than is the construction of a single stadium. In the bidding to host large events such as the World Cup or the Olympic Games, the battle of the cities takes on a global dimension. 'The fight for the Olympics lays the competition between the world cities out in the open,' Deyan Sudjic wrote.[24]

Nowadays, with a good strategic plan, the Olympics can also be a big money earner.[25] Baron de Coubertin, whose efforts gave the Olympic Games a new lease of life at the end of the nineteenth century, clearly bore both these aspects in mind. He was also able to convince the wealthy Greek businessmen that sponsoring the Olympic Games was a worthwhile investment, and the Olympic Games were resurrected in Athens in 1896, for the first time in 2000 years.

During the Olympic Games, the eyes of the whole world are turned towards the host city. The Olympics are increasingly seen as an opportunity to effect large-scale urban regeneration projects, using the extra monies that national governments bestow on a city which is to host the Olympics. The cities of Seoul (1988) and Barcelona (1992) used the Olympic Games as a reason for far-reaching urban renewal. Seoul spent $1.66 billion for facilities directly related to the Olympics, and a further $1.35 billion for the improvement of sanitary facilities, infrastructure (the capacity of the airport was doubled and an extra 200 kilometres – 125 miles – of track were added to the urban rail system), and the urban environment in general.[26] The city authorities drew up the plans with the support of national government, but it was the private sector that provided a large part of the investment. The city of Seoul was thus transformed with funds from the government and private businesses. Seoul built new sports facilities but, even more important, it constructed a complete Olympic Village. The Village, designed by Woo & Williams Architects, also served as an excuse to demolish dilapidated flats in a densely populated suburb, and replace them with new offices and flats. After the Olympic Games, the extensive village with a spacious, central square was used as standard housing for about 25,000 people. The building that had housed the dining facilities for the athletes during the Olympics was converted into a shopping

centre. The Olympic Games were also a political success for South Korea, because they showed the world that the politic situation was under control. From the very moment that Seoul was chosen as the host for the 1988

Olympic Games, the city started a campaign – and a successful one at that – in order to prevent the kind of boycott that Moscow had seen during the 1980 Olympic Games.

Another example of urban transformation as a spin-off from the Olympic Games is the city of Barcelona, which hosted the Olympics in 1992. Barcelona was no stranger to urban transformation in preparation for a large event: just over a century earlier, the city had also undergone a metamorphosis for the World Exhibition of 1888. 'With the boost of the fair, Barcelona was able to transform the overcrowding of its ramshackle, multilayered, medieval core into a modern city in a single generation.'27

Barcelona had already started working on urban regeneration in the 1980s, ridding itself of the dictatorial architecture of the Franco era, and the hosting of the Olympics was an ideal complement to this. 1981 saw the launch of 76 urban reconstruction projects, including the laying out of 150 squares.28 The Olympic Games was a further stimulus for Barcelona to take this metamorphosis further. The critic Peter Buchanan notes: 'It is rather difficult to recall the city of only a decade and a half ago.'29 Four key areas were designated for pre-Olympics development, and thus also as part of the city's permanent metamorphosis: Montjuic (Olympic stadium and other facilities), Nova Icara (the Olympic Village), Valle Hebron (press village, tennis courts, cycling and volleyball) and the Diagonale (the existing football and polo fields next to the university). The most impressive part of the whole plan was the construction of the Olympic Village in a run-down section of the city. The way in which this Olympic Village was developed was similar to the approach in Seoul. The Village was built on a former industrial zone on the waterfront, a strip that had always formed a barrier between the heart of the city and the sea. Barcelona had nursed ambitions to profile itself as a city by the sea since the 1960s, and in the 1980s this dream could at last be realized, thanks to the Olympics. The planners set the following objectives for the Olympic Village: the existing coastal railway would run underground; polluted water had to be cleaned up; beaches had to be created, and the whole area made more accessible by laying roads and establishing a public transport infrastructure. Oriol Bohigas was the leading light among the architects responsible for the project: Martorell/Bohigas/Mackay/Puigdomenech. As in Seoul, the village was intended to be integrated as a new district in post-Olympics Barcelona. Unfortunately, the demolition of most of the industrial buildings eradicated the history of the area, architecture historian

Olympic Village in Seoul, 1988

Josep Maria Montaner claimed: 'The Olympic Village stands as an area without referents, in the middle of a desert.'30 Alongside the work on the Olympic Village, other construction included hotels, theatres, cultural centres, a museum designed by Richard Meier, a concert hall by Rafael Moneo, a meteorological centre by Alvaro Siza, and an extension to the airport.

Looking at these two examples it is not surprising that Manchester and Amsterdam were not selected to host the Olympic Games. The budget that Manchester was willing to set aside for the 1996 Olympics was a fraction

of that proposed by other candidates, and Amsterdam initially wanted to treat the 1992 Olympics as a modest affair. They were unable to envisage a convincing image of a city ready to undergo a complete transformation.

Candidate cities are expected to pull out all the stops, and most cities are more than pleased to seize this opportunity. Johannesburg, which made a pitch for the 2000 Olympic Games, is an example of a city that saw the chance to host the Olympic Games in a broader context than just the hosting a sports event. If Johannesburg had won the race then the city would have been

Olympic Village in Barcelona, 1992

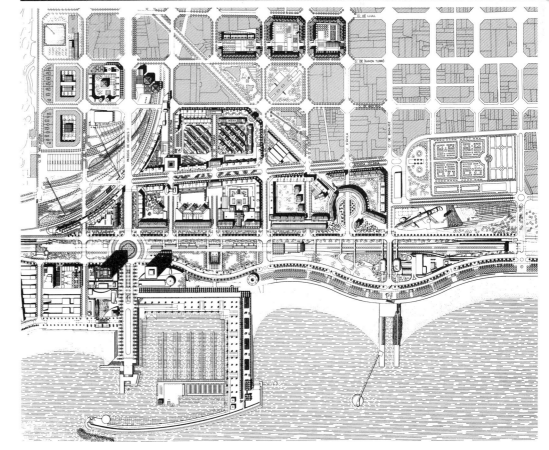

able to show the whole world the changes that had been brought about since the end of apartheid. In 1993 the city developed ten plans for the regeneration of different parts of the city, including of course a new Olympic stadium. Although Sydney won the race for the 2000 Olympics, the multifunctional athletics stadium in Johannesburg, to a 1995 design by Ove Arup Associates, was still realized. Johannesburg has to contend with a high level of crime and poverty, and the city hopes that this new stadium will help to change the urban climate. The stadium is available for activities for the whole community, for example religious festivals and charity events or benefit concerts, as well as for sports events. The city wanted to establish a new direction and leave behind the apartheid era, when only the whites came to the stadia, and blacks were banned from taking part in professional sport. The new stadium is not simply intended to herald a new period in a local sense, but it is also meant to embody an international allure. It marks the eradication of the years of the international sport boycott and a return to the international sports circuit. The planning of this stadium involved a complex balancing of economic, social and political objectives.

Athletics stadium in Johannesburg, 1995

'For whom are we saving the cities?'

Stadia do not just have a symbolic function in the improvement of a city's image; they also play an economic and political role. They are used as pump-primers for the creation of a recreation or leisure district, as the first step in the establishment of a new centre of economic activity, or – as with the hosting of the Olympic Games – as the pretext and opportunity for structural renewal of a whole city. But does this always succeed? The expensive stadia are often seen as a catalyst for the regeneration of a city or an urban district, but it can also turn out that the public funds would have been better spent in other ways.

These massive colossuses do not always sit so easily in their surroundings and, because

they accommodate so many commercial activities, it is also difficult to bring about any interaction with these immediate surroundings. Nevertheless, project developers and planners make repeated references to the alleged positive impact of the construction of modern stadia on the surrounding areas. The regeneration argument is often used, in Europe and the United States, to obscure the real incentive, which, more often than not, is a case of profit or political prestige. The

question posed by the sociologist Gregory Squires is very germane: 'For whom are we saving the cities?'[31]

1. www.fieldofschemes.com.
2. Nick Hornby, Fever Pitch (London: Victor Gollanz Ltd. 1992), p. 219.
3. Ibid., p. 221.
4. This is still often the case, for example in Milan (Inter FC and AC Milan) and the Amsterdam ArenA (Ajax and Admirals).
5. Steven A. Riess, City Games. The Evolution of American Urban Society and the Rise of Sports (Urbana: University of Illinois Press 1991), p. 227.
6. Ibid., p. 248.
7. Michael N. Danielson, Home Team. Professional Sports and the American Metropolis (Princeton: Princeton University Press 1997), p. 102.
8. Joanna Cagan and Neil deMause, Field of Schemes: How the Great Stadium Swindle Turns Public Money into Private Profit (Monroe: Common Courage Press 1998), p. 36.
9. Ibid., p. 158-159.
10. Ibid., p. 29.
11. Dean V. Baim and Larry Sitsky, The Sports Stadium as a Municipal Investment (Westport: Greenwood Press 1994), p. 150.
12. J. Hannigan, Fantasy City. Pleasure and Profit in the Postmodern Metropolis (London: Routledge 1998), p. 194.
13. www.fans4stpaul.com.
14. www.fieldofschemes.com.
15. Simon Inglis, The Football Grounds of Europe (London: Willow Books 1990), p. 111.
16. L. Pignatti, 'Il piu grande stadio del mondo: lo Skydome di Toronto' (The biggest stadium in the world: the SkyDome in Toronto), Gomorra 3, 1998, p. 18.
17. M. Fuller, 'Amerikaans superdome-concept voor a fractie van de prijs'

(The American superdome concept for a fraction of the price), Het Financieele Dagblad, August 2, 1996.
18. Ibid.
19. M. van den Broek, 'Arena blijft nog jarenlang bouwterrein' (The Arena will be a building site for years), de Volkskrant. August 7, 1996.
20. Prior to the selection of the Saint Denis location, EuroDisney was approached about a possible collaboration, but did not take up the offer. The choice of the Saint Denis site meant that the idea of the stadium forming part of a comprehensive recreation and amusement area came unstuck.
21. Dossier de presse du Stade de France (Press folder of the Stade de France), June 1998, p. 9.
22. Hannigan, p. 2.
23. Ibid., p. 147.
24. Deyan Sudjic, The 100 Mile City (Orlando: Harcourt Brace 1992), p. 240.
25. In Montreal this did not exactly go as planned: taxpayers were still paying for the Olympic stadium many years after the 1976 event.
26. B.P.M. Waters, 'Run-up to the 88 Olympics', Building, October 18, 1995, p. 49.
27. Sudjic, p. 204.
28. Rein Geurtsen, 'Labyrintisch landschap, laboratorium van stadsontwerp' (Labyrinthian landscape, a laboratory for urban design), Archis 11. November 1989, p. 35.
29. Peter Buchanan, 'Barcelona, a city regenerated', Architectural Review 1146, 1992, p. 11.
30. J.M. Montaner, 'L'idea del Villaggio olimpico di Barcelona. Tipi e morfologie' (The Olympic Village in Barcelona. Types and Morphologies), Lotus 67, 1990, p. 25.
31. Hannigan, p. 8.

Anywhere

Stadio San Nicola

name: Stadio San Nicola
place: Bari, Italy
date of construction: 1990
architects: Renzo Piano and Joseph Zucker
capacity: 58,000

Just outside the southern Italian city of Bari, an alien spaceship has alighted in the middle of the dry Apulian olive grove landscape. Especially at night, when the solitary saucer is dramatically illuminated from below, the colossus appears to hover. This alien intruder is the San Nicola football stadium.

The huge oval shell balances on an artificially green hill in which a crater has been carved out for the first tier of seats and for an athletic track around the actual playing field. Immediately below this first tier (in the ground, in other words) are all the changing rooms and service areas. The hill also forms a green buffer around the stadium and in order not to disrupt this effect, an underground road was built around the entire stadium so that players coaches, police cars and ambulances are completely separated from spectators.

Piano divided the concrete tier above into 26 compartments. In between he created recesses from which 'gangplanks' fold down to connect up with the radial paths leading to the car park. This was done partly for security reasons (to break up the crowd) but also to establish a relationship with the surrounding landscape. The resulting transparent stadium is a total departure from the wholly enclosed, classical Roman arena.

The roof of transparent Teflon panels follows the height differences of the second ring of seating in a graceful, wave-like motion. On the outside, Piano has emphasized the parabolic curve of the stand sections and made no attempt to conceal this. The elegant structure, the light roof and the barely visible columns all conspire to give the impression of a spaceship ready to depart at a moment's notice.

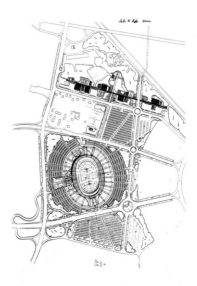

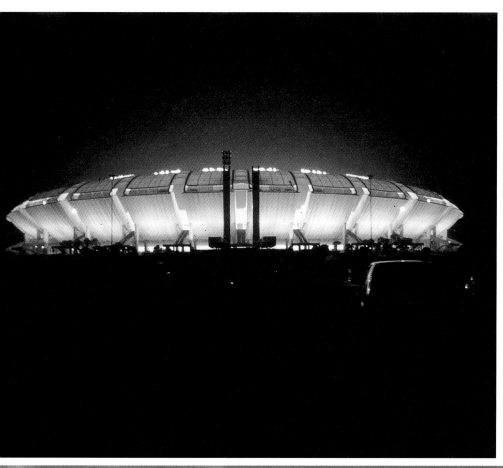
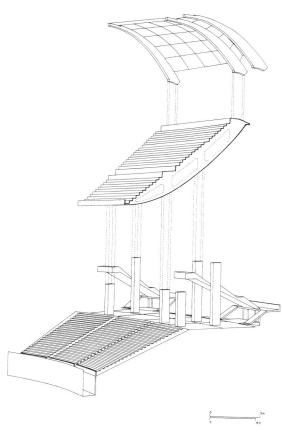

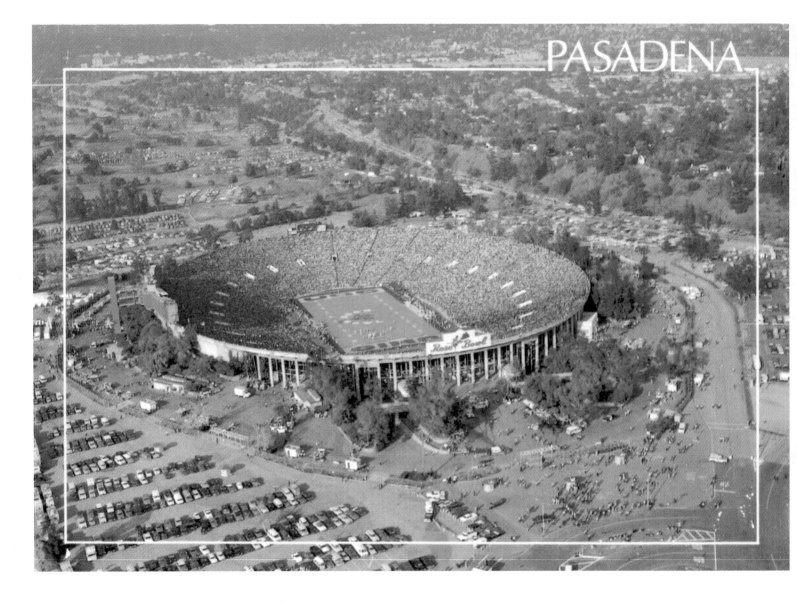

Rose Bowl

name: Rose Bowl
place: Pasadena, United States
date of construction: 1920-1923
architect: Myron Hunt
capacity: 91,000

The United States has many big stadia, both multi-purpose and stadia built specifically for baseball or American football which are usually referred to as Concrete Doughnuts or Concrete Bowls. One of the most famous Bowls stands on the campus of the University of California where, every New Year's Day since 1902, the Tournament of Roses which has been held. This festival consists of a parade and a football match between the championship teams of the Big Ten and Pacific Ten Conferences and the Rose Bowl was built specifically to house it. Architect Myron Hunt and engineer William A. Taylor designed a horseshoe-shaped stadium for 57,000 spectators, the first match being played there in 1923.

The popularity of the match grew and the stadium grew with it. In 1928 the open south side was filled in, raising the capacity to 76,000 spectators. Later additions (1932, 1949 and 1972) raised the capacity to 105,000. Since then modifications aimed at increasing spectator comfort, such as the introduction of plastic bucket seats, have reduced the capacity to around 91,000.

The stands run in a single unbroken ring around the field which is sunken so that spectators enter the stadium half-way up the stands. On the outside, the stands are supported by concrete columns that form an almost classic colonnade.

Dodger Stadium

name: Dodger Stadium
place: Los Angeles, United States
date of construction: 1959-1962
architects: Praeger, Kavanagh & Waterbury
capacity: 56,000

What soccer is to Europeans and Latin Americans, baseball and gridiron are to Americans. Just about every American is formally or emotionally attached to a club whose players enjoy superstar status. Baseball stadia, with their characteristic horseshoe shape, have a smaller capacity than enclosed arenas. The V-shaped stands follow the layout of the baseball pitch: because most of the play is concentrated around one spot, few stadia bother with an outfield stand; from that distance there would be very little to see.

The Dodger Stadium is the outcome of a remarkable rebellion that took place in the baseball world of the 1950s. Two of the top teams, the Dodgers and the Giants, decided to swap New York for Los Angeles and San Francisco respectively. Both had been based in very old stadia – the Polo Grounds (1911) and Yankee Stadium (1923) – that were in urgent need of refurbishment. When the City of New York put too many obstacles in the way of their rebuilding plans they simply upped sticks and moved to California.

The Dodger Stadium stands on the outskirts of Los Angeles surrounded by a sea of asphalt with parking spaces for 16,000 cars. It is a baseball stadium with one big V-shaped stand and two lower stands behind the outfield. The main stand consists of three tiers, the first of which is below ground level. The prime viewing section behind home plate has an additional fourth tier. Because there is a high risk of earthquakes in this area the main stand is composed of several freestanding elements.

As was customary for stadia of the period, Dodger Stadium is a mono-functional sports venue: baseball is the only sport played here. In recent decades, however, the stadium has hosted more and more non-sporting events. The Rolling Stones and U2 are only two of the acts to have performed here. In 1987 Pope John Paul II even celebrated mass in the National League ballpark.

Amsterdam ArenA

Name: Amsterdam ArenA
place: Amsterdam, the Netherlands
date of construction: 1993-1996
architects: Rob Schuurman
and Sjoerd Soeters
capacity: 51,324

Rob Schuurman deliberately gave the stadium the appearance of a flying saucer, a striking silhouette with a curved roof. The monster's landing place in Amsterdam Southeast seems fairly fortuitous; it could just as well have alighted anywhere else in the urban periphery.

Where Schuurman thinks in spatial forms, Sjoerd Soeters, who was called in during the final phase of the design to resolve objections raised by the local Design Review Committee, thinks in associations. He redesigned the stairtowers, giving them round holes and diagonal cross connections, like laces in a football boot. In front of the end stairtowers he placed a concrete slab with holes 'you could kick a ball through'. He added a plinth to a height of 8.40 metres below which there is room for numerous commercial uses and he designed the gate-house building over Burgemeester Stramanweg in his well-known postmodernist Rolex architecture.

The stadium sits on top of a huge car park. The two cantilevered, all-seater stands are served by three galleries which also contain the toilet and catering facilities. A notable feature, apart from the imposing high-tech roof construction, is the emphasis placed on customer care, service and comfort: luxury tip-up seats, a roof that keeps all spectators dry and many easy-to-reach amenities. The reason is that Amsterdam ArenA was designed as a multi-purpose events venue. Two panels move over two roof trusses to close off the stadium completely.

As the first European stadium to opt for a sliding roof, ArenA has been plagued by an almost chronic teething problem: the grass simply will not grow. With the roof in the open position, the opening is exactly the same size as the pitch below so that too little direct daylight falls on the turf and the air circulation in the stadium is inadequate for growth. The highly expensive turf has been replaced so often that people are beginning to lose count.

Intervie

Zwarts & Jans

'A football stadium is a

Moshé Zwarts and Rein Jansma set up Zwarts & Jansma Architecten in 1990. They have been involved in the renovation of the Feyenoord Stadium (1994, in collaboration with Van den Broek & Bakema), and Galgenwaard Stadium (c. 2004) and built the new Sparta Stadium (1999). At present they are working on the new Omniworld sport and leisure complex in Almere which is due to be completed in 2002.

What is the challenge in designing a stadium?
Rein Jansma: The challenge is that when all's said and done, a football stadium is a completely useless building because you're much better off watching football on television. It's a building dedicated to the emotion of 'being there'. An incredible amount of money is reserved for a stadium that is only used once a week for a couple of hours maximum. It's a marvellous challenge to design a building for this phenomenon. On top of this, more and more functions have been clustered in the stadium in recent years and this makes the building more complex. People have come to understand that it's actually rather a shame to go to the stadium only to leave again immediately after the match. What can you do to an existing stadium to turn it into a multi-purpose building? What's more, a stadium is a big structure with a fair amount of repetition. This means that you can optimize small components. The fact that a particular component

crops up so frequently makes it economically significant and that helps you to convince clients and producers of the need for change.

What are the most important developments at this point in time?
The size of the pitch determines quite a lot of things in advance. There is one development, however, and that is the trend towards a movable pitch that sinks into the ground, slides away horizontally, turns into a ceiling or is rolled up. This is going to become increasingly important. That will have quite an effect on stadium design. And there'll be artificial grass. It's not clear yet when exactly but everyone hopes that it will be relatively soon because it allows a lot of design freedom. Artificial grass will be a tremendous advance.

I think that in future the emphasis is going be more on the pitch than on the roof. When you have a pitch like the one in the Gelredome that can be pushed back and forth, the opening and closing of the roof won't matter any more.

The stadium is not going to disappear in the future even though television technology has reduced the need for a stadium. Sitting in front of the television with a group of friends and a crate of beer is all very nice, but there's still a big demand for a stadium as such. After all, the essence is

w with

a Architecten

bletely useless building'

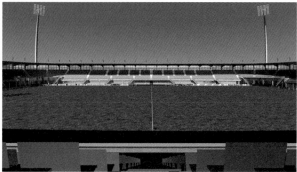

3   4   5

that you are able to smell the sweat and rub shoulders with other people. Introducing a monitor for every visitor with all kinds of information will not alter the essential nature of the visit to the stadium. I don't see that as a fundamental change. For my money the movable pitch and a totally roofed-in building are the two most important developments.

Is a stadium linked specifically to an area or is it autonomous?
Stadium design is first and foremost a matter of logistics. How do the visitors circulate, where does public transport and ordinary traffic come from? Then you create a place using these data. Feyenoord Stadium, for example, acts like a magnet. People converge on it from every direction but the residual space is not what you'd call convivial. We're trying to better that at Omniworld in Almere. The stadium here is only one part of the whole; football is only an hour and a half out of the four or five hours spent on recreation. You have 15,000 visitors and what are you going to offer them? You can see that all sorts of activities have been incorporated into it so that the stadium turns into a leisure park. It is a place that takes full account of the railway line, access via the station

1. Roof structure Feyenoord Stadium in Rotterdam, 1994

2. Home of History in Feyenoord Stadium

3. Renovation of Galgenwaard Stadium in Utrecht, 2004

4. Provisional design for Omniworld Stadium in Almere, 1999

5. Renovation of Galgenwaard Stadium in Utrecht, 2004

6. Provisional design for Omniworld Stadium in Almere, 1999

and the car, parking spaces and bus routes. But it is also much more than a place. It is a sort of street you can walk through, with shops on either side and a range of activities. You can enter an enclosure with an automatic baseball pitcher or tennis server or football simulation. The boundary between media and reality is becoming blurred. I see it as an important development that you think primarily in terms of logistics and at the same time make sure that the place itself becomes an enjoyable place to be. This building could theoretically be erected anywhere as long as the programme remains the same.

A stadium expresses the significance of sport. To what extent does this apply to contemporary stadia?
I think that football was a much more demotic and less socially divided event in the 1930s. At Sparta, even though it was a gents' club, everyone just stood around the pitch together. Society was much more hierarchical then and perhaps sport was something that united people. Now you find separate sections being created for each target group. It's not just corporate seats and corporate suites, but a special guest section, a section for the scouts and trainers of the other club, players'

wives, the press, relatives, the local supporters' club and finally local visitors. With a bit of effort, even the supporters in the guest section could be put in a separate section. But there is no demand for that. Obviously there is such a thing as a 'feeling of togetherness', but 15,000 plus spectators is too much for that. So they are split up into smaller groups so that everybody has a stronger sense of affinity. This is a major change. I think it's motivated by more than just security considerations. There's another reason for dividing it up into parts. There's choice built into it, individually experienced space.

What will the stadium of the future look like? What new trends are likely?
In think that in thirty years' time today's minimum of 50,000 spectators for a major game will have been abandoned. People will come to realize that the experience and atmosphere are far more important, so that a more intimate pitch may be more appropriate. I wouldn't be surprised if the football pitch became much smaller. In America they're always complaining that so few goals are scored and that this makes it dull. If the pitch were much smaller scoring would be faster and soccer would move in the direction of indoor football. The whole game is going to be turned upside down and that will affect the pitch. In future it may be possible to nominate which players you think should be switched. It would be up to the trainer to decide, but it would give the spectators a measure of interaction. That would be a clear incentive to go to the match, because of the involvement. Perhaps it would no longer be just a matter of points scored but also appreciation for the game itself. When all's said and done it's about a theatrical performance with suspense and emotion rather than the number of points someone has scored. Beauty will be more highly rated and the fact that you are all there together. Now the only means of expression are yelling, shouting and waving flags, but in future you'll be able to use this console to record your appreciation of a superb bit of play and at the end of the game you'll vote for the player of the match.

If you want to increase contact with the public, a stadium seating 50,000 people is too big. The ideal is a small pitch with 1,000 to 10,000 people seated around it in high, steeply raked stands so that they are all close to the pitch. The game can just as easily take place in a hall then instead of outside. The hall becomes part of a spectacle, it is part of a shopping mall. The family wants to do something together on their Saturday off but they all have different interests. So the husband goes to the football, the wife to the garden centre next door and the children go off to McDonald's

mammoth 50-metre ball pool. At five o'clock they all meet up again to try out one of the restaurants located around the place. This way watching football becomes just one part of a day out. The stadium will lose its own sculptural, autonomous form. It will shrink in size and disappear inside a building. What does an Albert Heijn supermarket look like for instance? An Albert Heijn has no exterior but is tucked away inside a big block. At this point you can't really tell the difference between a big leisure pool and a shopping mall. They're all tin boxes with atria and inside there can be all sorts of things. Such complexes don't have a specific form any more so they are less and less recognizable from outside – they dissolve as it were.

6

First

Astrodome

name: Astrodome
place: Houston, United States
date of construction: 1961-1965
architects: Lloyd & Morgan; Wilson,
Morris & Anderson
capacity: 55,000 (baseball) –
70,000 (concerts)

The Harris County Domed Stadium, to give the Astrodome its official name, was the world's first multi-purpose, roofed stadium. It is located close to downtown Houston and encircled by a car park with spaces for 30,000 cars. The almost 70-metre-high dome, which protects the public from sun, rain and mosquitoes, was based on the 'geodesic dome' of architect-engineer Richard Buckminster Fuller. The dome rests on a circular substructure with a diameter of almost 215 metres and consists of steel slats and trusses that together form a lattice framework. The diamond-shaped openings between the slats were originally filled with transparent plastic panes but the bright light made it impossible for the baseball players to discern flyballs. When experiments with sunglasses and orange-coloured balls failed to solve the problem, it was decided to paint the panes a semi-opaque white. As a result the grass refused to grow and in 1966 it had to be replaced by the now famous artificial grass known as Astroturf™.

A major renovation, completed in 1989, has raised the level of amenities in the stadium. Among other things, 66 luxury suites and 12 super suites were added. The stadium was also provided with a 'Magic Carpet': two separate playing fields, one for baseball and one for American Football, are stored in basements underneath the arena and rolled out as needed.

Stadion Galgenwaard

name: Stadion Galgenwaard
place: Utrecht, the Netherlands
date of construction: 1977-1982
architect: Ballast Nedam
capacity: 20,000

Galgenwaard Stadium was a pioneer in the field of stadium safety and multi-functionality. Its architect, Ballast Nedam, employed architectural devices in an effort to combat football hooliganism. While there are no barriers around the ground, a sunken corridor (the moat) makes it practically impossible for spectators to invade the pitch. In nearly all stadia, the terraces behind the goals are the places favoured by the most fanatical football fans. Traditionally, these standing room areas are the cheapest part of the stadium and usually so crowded that it is difficult for police and stewards to patrol them. Galgenwaard broke with this tradition by filling the areas behind the goal with proper seating.

Another novelty in terms of European stadium construction was the fact that the building of the stadium was financed by the incorporation of 30,000 m² office space. The offices are located in the corners (with a view of the pitch), between the four individual covered stands on each side of the ground and also underneath the stands.

The architects Zwarts & Jansma have recently produced plans aimed at modernizing the stadium. The success of the original multi-functional approach is demonstrated by the rise in the number of square metres commercial space and the addition of 48 hospitality boxes.

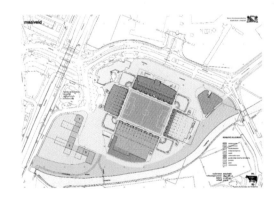

Gelredome

name: Gelredome
place: Arnhem, the Netherlands
date of construction: 1996-1998
architect: Alynia
capacity: 27,000

From the outside, Arnhem's multi-function sports and events venue looks for all the world like an exhibition centre or auction hall. There is nothing to suggest a glorious football temple where hard-won victories are notched up and famous players score fantastic goals. Even the light masts, the totem poles of soccer, are lacking: because of the closable roof the lighting unit has been integrated with the roofing above the stands. The Gelredome is a square box surmounted by two bulges (the moving sections of the roof) and surrounded by an anony-mous glazed façade.

The four stands are fitted with blocks of seats in a wide variety of bright colours. The corners are infilled with highly visible concrete walls that divide the stadium into four com-partments and in so doing prevent the public from ever merging into a single whole.

The Gelredome was built in order to give Arnhem a public attraction with inter-national allure. The technical innovations, such as the retractable roof, contribute to this. The stadium also boasts an ingenious system of climate con-trol.

In winter it is pleasantly warm and in summer delightfully cool. The most revolu-tionary feature of the Vitesse Football Club's home ground, however, is the mobile pitch. This lies outside the stadium where it receives sufficient air and sunlight to keep the grass in prime condition. Events are staged on the concrete subfloor. Then, before a football match, the southern stand swings upwards and the turf is slowly rolled into the stadium on an ingenious system of teflon plates developed by Ballast Nedam.

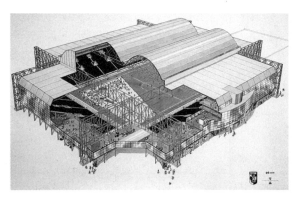

Kitakyushu Media Dome

name: Kitakyushu Media Dome
place: Fukuoka, Japan
date of construction: 1996-1998
architect: Kikutake Architects
capacity: 20,000

The Media Dome stands in the middle of Kitakyushu, a city in the process of transforming itself from an urban economy based on industry into an international centre of information science. The stadium has an important role to play in this process for although it includes an arena for sporting events, large sections of the building have been designed with an eye to multimedia entertainment and information transfer. For example, there is an Alice Lab, where high-tech machinery allows visitors to experience for themselves the celebrated Alice in Wonderland story. There is a Media Loop, a route around the outside of the stands, that is filled with monitors providing a wide range of information and access to the Internet. And there is a Multi Vision Hall with a five-metre-wide screen for all manner of shows and presentations. The monitor in the arena itself is a gigantic 24 metres wide, so that spectators can follow every detail of the cycle race, sumo wrestling match or concert on the screen. More than any other sports stadium, the Media Dome is a blend of media and sport.

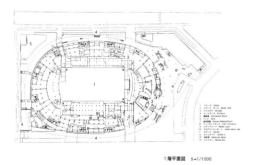

1階平面図　S=1/1000

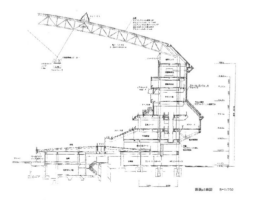

断面1断面図　S=1/750

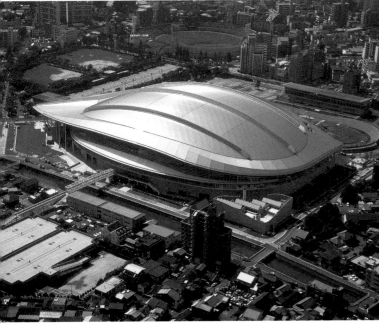

Toronto SkyDome

name: Toronto SkyDome
place: Toronto, Canada
date of construction: 1986-1989
architects: RAN Consortium, Rod Robbie,
Mike Allen & Bill Neish
capacity: 55,000 (baseball) –
70,000 (concerts)

As the first stadium in the world with a fully retractable roof, the Toronto SkyDome presented the designers and engineers with a big technical challenge. The resulting roof consists of four panels, three of which rotate or slide in a complicated procedure until the roof is fully open (exposing 100% of the field and 91% of the seats). The three movable panels end up stacked on top of the stationary one at the north side of the stadium, so that no shadow falls on the artificial grass pitch.

The panels are composed of steel trusses spanning the width of the pitch. The trusses rest on bogies that move over a steel track mounted on the concrete substructure. Each bogey is individually driven so that in case of an electrical malfunction in one of the bogies, the roof can still be opened and closed.

The stadium is multi-purpose and the lowest tier of stands can be moved depending on whether Canadian Football, American Football, baseball, rugby or soccer is to be played there. Yet the number of sporting events pales into insignificance beside the 2,500 other events that have been held here since the opening: concerts, opera, 'demolition derbies', the three tenors, boat shows, religious festivals by Christians, Moslems and other faiths, political conventions, circus, carnival and so on.

The stadium is located close to the city centre and is part of a major redevelopment of the Toronto waterfront, with the CN Tower as landmark. The stadium boasts no fewer than 61 luxury sky boxes and a colossal ten by forty metre video display board. A unique feature is the four-star hotel built into the north end of the facility; of its 346 rooms, 70 enjoy a spectacular view of the arena.

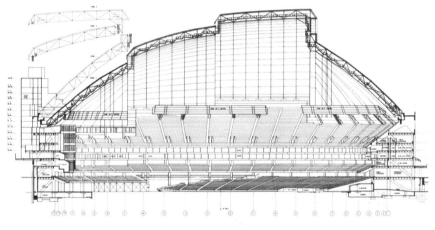

Fashion and personality

body

Biomechanics and artful sculpting help star athlete Aimee Mullins triumph on the track—and off. By Amy Goldwasser

DIESEL
FOOTWEAR

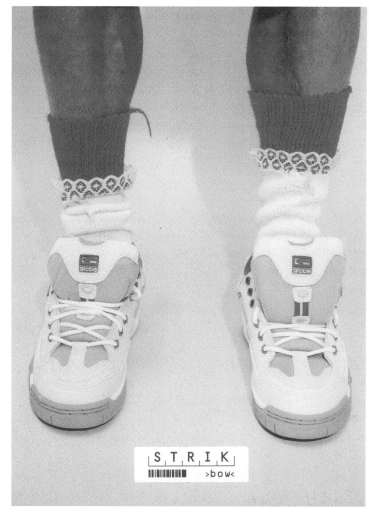

STRIK
>bow<

Sport an

Pauline

Tracksuits, body warmers, jogging pants, trainers – look around you on the street and you could be forgiven for thinking that just about every passer-by is engaged in some form of sport. Although the condescending 'camp-site formal' appellation does perhaps suggest that all that glitters is not gold. For 'camp-site formal' is a term most notably applied to those comfortable, pull-on outfits in stretch materials and jazzy colours that are worn by so many men nowadays – and not just around their mobile home or in front of the sports channel of their television set. The derogatory designation of this group's wardrobe is a way of saying that leisure wear sometimes makes for a rather monotonous street scene – just as a room full of men in black tie can be too much of a good thing, making one yearn for just one stand-out red sports shirt.

But is this disdain vis à vis sportswear really justified? Let's take a look at recent collections from the big international fashion labels. There's a collar fastened to the jacket edge with Velcro (Helmut Lang), a men's jacket in stretch material with back panels lengthened and rounded like a sports shirt (Armani), lace-up and clip fastenings for trousers and shirt (Prada), not to mention the ubiquitous horizontal or vertical stripes in contrasting fabrics or colours on sleeves and trouser-legs (copied from Adidas) – indeed, you would be hard put nowadays to find a fashion item that has not been influenced by sportswear. And that's just the most visible details. Anyone with any knowledge of fabrics knows that comfortable, stretchy, heat- and moisture-regulating fabrics (all originally developed for one branch of sport or another)

have an even greater impact on contemporary fashion. Even men's suits are nowadays made of the stretch Lycra that was originally designed for swim and skiwear. Not that the wearer is really intending to do a series of knee stretches, but the possibility is there. A similar case of functional overkill is the super hard-wearing fabric previously used by the motorcycling fraternity and now being applied to women's handbags: though not strictly necessary for a powder compact and lipstick, it does look authentically contemporary. In short, sport and fashion have merged completely over the course of the last hundred years.

There is no need to go into the history of this symbiosis in detail, but a few highlights may serve to refresh the memory. The biggest sporting impact on women's fashion was the craze for cycling in the late nineteenth century. When women suddenly had to use their legs to maintain their balance on two wheels, they no longer had any use for voluminous skirts. But it was not until after the Second World War that women completely revealed their slender silhouette under the influence of skiwear and the accompanying tight ski pants.

As for men, it was the nineteenth-century romantic outdoor life, with the now somewhat obsolete pleasures of the hunt, that freed them from the most restrictive elements of the black dress suit they were expected to wear whenever they appeared in public. In addition, football and tennis resulted in progressively looser and more elastic clothing. In essence this change, too, had its origins in the use of a particular type of fabric. Instead of woven fabrics, sports clothes

d fashion

reehorst

were made of thin, knitted fabrics. Originally they were used exclusively for underwear – at first men even played football in their combinations. Later on the knitting technique was refined and nowadays we know this fabric as the much smarter jersey.

The most important contribution to the marriage of sport and fashion, however, derives from the chemical industry. Without the constant invention of new synthetic fibres, sportswear fashion could not exist.

Looking at the trends for the future, there seems to be little likelihood of an early end to the golden alliance of sport and fashion. A more probable scenario is that there will soon be no difference at all between formal clothing for the office and sportswear for the leisure hours. It used to be that one of the secret pleasures of practising an exclusive sport (golf, skiing) was that it gave you a pretext for going out and buying an equally exclusive wardrobe. Nowadays every Tom, Dick and Harry walks around in a Helly Hansen sailing jacket, Tommy Hilfiger board shorts and, if they're lucky, a pair of the new, sock-like golden Nikes that could theoretically be used for jogging. The special sport with which one's outward appearance might be associated has become an irrelevancy. The important thing is not to look as if one is seriously contemplating doing something. For whether it's building an Internet site or spending an afternoon surfing, skating or snowboarding, it has to remain fun. For heaven's sake don't go getting excited. 'Be cool' is what these clothes say, a condition totally incompatible with sport when you come to think about it.

One development influencing this trend is the changed attitude to work in general, which is increasingly expected to be a combination of performance and entertainment. After the eighties, which saw both men and women donning crisply tailored suits (the age of power dressing), the nineties ushered in an era when, spurred on by favourable economic conditions, a more relaxed attitude was permissible. In the United States, Easy Friday greatly boosted the turnover of the likes of Ralph Lauren. In Europe it quickly turned into one long holiday. Nearly all the fashion labels developed a separate line to satisfy the new demand for comfort. The addition of the word 'jeans' (Armani Jeans, Gaultier Jeans, Versace Jeans) was not just an indication that these clothes cost only one-third as much as the 'top' line, the label also suggested a kind of comfort that had always been associated with sport. Which is why we are going to see even more faux sportsmanship in future. As soon as the laptop-toting hordes start flexi-working all over the place – at home, on the boat, in the caravan, or in their suburb-turned-amusement park – clothing will become more and more casual. So let's prepare ourselves for the worst: the most fashionable item of clothing in the future will be the loose-fitting bath robe in snazzy club colours – the kind you put on after a shower at the end of a bout of intense physical exertion. No one will be enquiring about scores or final times. It's the image that counts.

Intervie

Kajima C

'A strong awareness of the regio

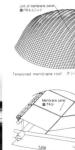

1 2 3 4

The Kajima corporation was established in 1840 as a construction company in Tokyo and has since then developed a practice with a wide range of specializations including sporting facilities. Nowadays Kajima employs over 13,000 people. The office focuses on improving technologies and creating new construction methods, as is clearly demonstrated by their stadia.

What is Kajima's experience with the design of sports buildings?

Masaru Ozaki (architect and general manager): From the seventies on we have been working on the development of membrane structures and large-scale compiled wood structures for the roofing over of stadia. We started to design and execute the construction of several stadia with a membrane structure in the eighties. Since the nineties we have realized a number of famous sports buildings, including the Akita Sky Dome (a community dome of 12,000 m² with a steel frame construction and a membrane roof in Akita), the Izumo Dome (a community dome of 16,000 m² with a compiled wood construction and a membrane roof in Izumo), the Yamabiko Dome (a community dome of 10,000 m² with a compiled wood construction and a metal roof in Matsumoto), the Nagano M-wave (the Nagona Olympic Memorial Arena of 70,000 m² with a compiled wood construction and a

metal roof) and the Seibu Dome (a baseball stadium of 40,000 m² with a steel-frame construction and a metal roof).

What would you describe as typical of the way Kajima designs sports buildings?

First of all, we design a stadium so that it functions as a sports building, while at the same time we also attach importance to its multi-functionality. This is not only because it facilitates a high rate of utilization, but also because it improves the balance in business. Secondly, we are very much concerned with the control of the stadium's interior environment. Conditions of sound, heat, light and wind must always be under control, and we also make the form of the building itself an energy-saving contrivance, which makes our design unique. Last but not least, we always design our buildings with a strong awareness of the regional character. The harmony of the building and its surroundings and the correspondence with regional climatic conditions are always taken into account. These are the characteristics that distinguish our work from that of others.

Which stadium is Kajima most proud of?

There are two projects I would like to mention. The first one is the Nagano M-Wave stadium and the other is the Seibu

w with

rporation

:haracter and climate conditions'

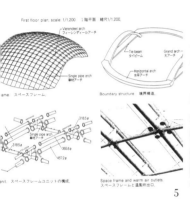

First floor plan; scale: 1/1.200 1階平面 縮尺1/1.200.

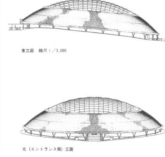

北（エントランス側）立面

5　　　　　　　　　6　　　　　　　　　7　　　　　　　　　8

Dome. Nagano M-Wave is actually the Nagona Olympic Memorial Arena. It was the Nagano Olympic speed skating venue in 1998 and at the same time, the space has been divided in such a way that the stadium can also be used for other, smaller regional events. It contains various kinds of changeable devices to cope with usage after the Olympic games. It has received wide recognition both in Japan and internationally. In 1997 it was awarded a gold medal by the British Institution of Structural Engineers for its unique form and its functionality. In 1999 it received another gold medal from IOC/IAKS.

1-3. Izumo Dome in Izumo, 1992

4-5. Akita Skydome in Yuwa-machi, 1989

6-7. Seibu Dome in Seibu, 1997

8. Nagano Olympic Memorial Arena in Nagano, 1996

The other project is Seibu Dome. It was originally an open-air baseball stadium. We are proud of it because not even one day of softball matches was lost while the roof was being built. The idea of using the two off-season periods for the construction makes it the first example in the world where a new roof has been built on an open-air stadium while the original stadium was totally untouched. We can say that this renovation inhabited the complete history of the original stadium. It is an environmental symbiotic type of dome, which doesn't bear the burden of air conditioning. Breaking with the heavily equipped

type of domes that are being built all over the world, this is another new building type for the next generation.

What is the biggest challenge in the design of a stadium?

When we design such a space, the biggest challenge is to control the sound, heat, light and wind conditions of the interior into a passive, sustainable state by means of its form. I think it is necessary to develop the technology of construction and equipment in order to fulfil this ideal of a sustainable building.

What has been the influence of safety regulations?

It is important to have concepts of structural safety and disaster prevention. On the aspect of structural safety, for example, we have to consider wind load, earthquake load etc.; in the field of disaster prevention we take care of fire incidence restraints, prevention of ignition, combustion, smoke accumulation, emergency evacuation etc. We have been developing all these techniques with simulation methods.

Does the stadium have a public meaning and how is this visualized?

A stadium, being a facility for the community, obviously is part of public space. It has a strong character deriving from its being part of urban planning. As architects, we are expected to contribute to the local community and it is our responsibility to respond to this expectation. We do so by designing multi-functional sports buildings. Also the surroundings of such a facility are designed to be open to the local public as much as possible.

Do you think there is a big difference between Asia and Europe in the design of sports buildings?

The big difference between stadium design in Asia and in Europe lies in the solutions to the differences in climate. In Asia (including Japan), a climate of high temperatures and high humidity makes it extremely difficult to control the hot and wet conditions in a large space like a stadium. I believe this makes the design of a stadium in Asia a tougher job.

The favourite stadium of... *C.M. Ottevanger*

Chief of Police for the Rotterdam-Rijnmond area

'The most beautiful football stadium in the Netherlands is De Kuip in Rotterdam. Not simply because countless football matches have been played here, but also because of the enormous number of pop concerts that attract hundreds of thousands of fans to this sports temple every year.

Stadium and police share a common interest here: the safety of every visitor. Safety is also the issue that has brought the stadium and the police together for the European Football Championships in the summer of 2000. I am sure that the safety and security measures will also contribute to making this a fantastic tournament, culminating in an inimitable final in De Kuip on July 2nd!'

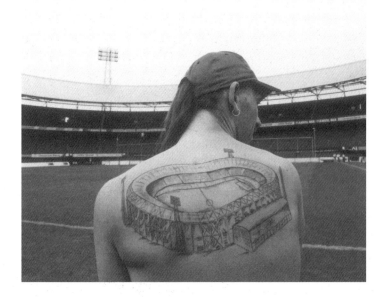

New

Miyagi Prefectural Stadium

name: Miyagi Prefectural Stadium
place: Miyagi, Japan
date of construction: 1992-2000
architects: Hitoshi Abe with Syouichi Hariu
capacity: 50,000

Traditional stadia have a geometric, closed form with a clear distinction between inside and out. Inspired by the hilly setting, Hitoshi Abe has designed Miyagi Stadium as an open structure that is a combination of stadium and park. Both programmes have been interwoven, allowing the building to develop into a three-dimensional park.

The elements of the stadium have been deconstructed and reassembled in an asymmetrical, scenographic relationship. The stands are open at the rear so that they appear to float unsupported. They are covered by two differently shaped roofs. The one on the side facing the hills is the taller and larger of the two and together they ensure that the stadium, built of plain, natural-coloured concrete, merges almost imperceptibly with its surroundings.

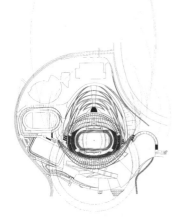

Sapporo Dome

name: Sapporo Dome
place: Sapporo, Japan
date of construction: 1998-2001
architects: Hiroshi Hara
capacity: 42,000

The Sapporo Dome is one of the many stadia being built for World Cup series to be held in Japan and Korea in 2002. As well as spawning a boom in stadium construction they are stimulating the development of many new technical innovations.

In 1996, the city of Sapporo, with 1.8 million inhabitants the largest city in northern Japan, held a competition for a multi-purpose stadium that was won by Hiroshi Hara with a design for a 'double arena'. A movable roof was virtually out of the question in an area of high snowfall so in order to meet the need for a natural turf football pitch, Hara opted instead for a movable pitch. Two arenas have been pushed together, one outside and the other under cover. The football pitch can move between the two by means of a high-tech system that uses air pressure to raise the pitch and then wheel it to the other arena. The pitch can also rotate so that spectators are always close to the action whether the game being played is baseball or football.

Above the large opening in the dome, through which the pitch can be rolled outside, is a restaurant. It has views of matches inside and outside the Dome and of the tree-filled park complete with botanical gardens that is to be laid out around the stadium.

Even after the World Cup the stadium will continue to play an important role as an events venue and as the focus of the park.

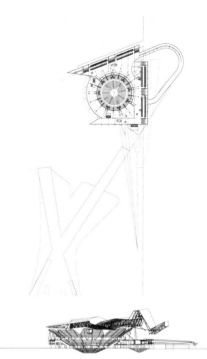

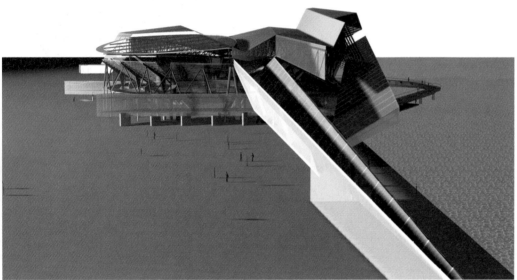

Palenque/Centro JVC

name: Palenque/Centro JVC
place: Guadalajara, Mexico
date of design: 1999
architect: Morphosis
capacity: 6,250

In traditional Mexican culture, the palenque is the place where the spectacular cockfights are held. Nowadays they are increasingly a venue for other events, such as boxing matches, public gatherings and traditional folk concerts. Cockfights, which are still legal in Mexico, are catered for in this stadium in a small, intimate auditorium dug into the ground around a small podium. Because it is uncertain how long such fights will continue to be an important cultural ritual, the stadium allows for a transformation by means of a floor laid over the small arena whereby it can be used for sporting events. The structure is a combination of an orthogonal grid which dominates the lower levels and a radial structure above this. Poised on top of the massive and primitive lower levels is a light and technologically sophisticated superstructure. The bowl-shaped arena is borne on a forest of irregularly forked columns.

The roof is conceived as a continuation of the landscape and reflects quite explicitly the surrounding folds and hills. It consists of a mesh of lattice girders over which a translucent membrane is laid. The solidarity with the environment is reinforced by the fact that two levels have been left quite open and devoid of programme thus providing unobstructed views out of the arena to the surrounding countryside.

Cardinals Stadium
Arizona Exposition and Convention Center Rio Salado Crossing

name: Cardinale Stadium (Arizona Exposition
and Convention Center Rio Salado Crossing)
place: Mesa, Arizona
date of design: 1998
architect: Peter Eisenman
capacity: 63,000

Mesa, not far from the state capital Phoenix, has long been regarded as a dull dormitory town. Now that the population has reached 400,000 it feels the need for an identity and amenities of its own. The Rio Salado Crossing project is a multi-functional development intended to furnish Mesa with the 'postcard image' it desires.

The core of the project is a huge convention centre with two 1250-room hotels and an NFL stadium that can be enlarged to accommodate 80,000 spectators for Super Bowls and other mega events. Eisenman has freed the stadium from its traditional static form and produced a design of flowing lines and curves. The roof sections are asymmetrical and reach tentacle-like into the surrounding area. They cover not just the stands but also numerous other functions, including the convention centre. The stadium has a movable pitch that can be rolled inside on match days. Where the two roof section touch is an oculus that allows light to enter the stadium through a movable glazed roof.

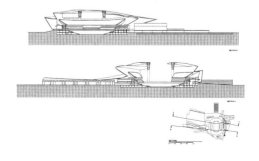

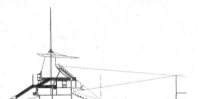
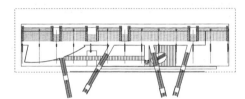
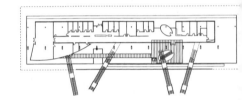

Tribunes d'honneur parc des sports des Montées

name: Tribunes d'honneur parc des
sports des Montées
place: Orléans, France
date of design: 1997
architect: Odile Decq
capacity: 1,750

Owing to the grandstand's location in the flood plain of the Loire, a river that is prone to flooding, it was decided to place the building on a plinth. The plinth is incorporated into an embankment, a green slope that supports a stand on the side facing the pitch. Furthermore, two tunnels have been dug either side of the structure to carry away excess water.

The fragmented and asymmetrical shape of the stand is inspired by the dynamics, force and speed of the rugby game. The seats are spread over two separate tiers, the lower of which rests on the embankment while the upper tier serves to crown the structure. In between is a level with facilities for players, press and television and another containing corporate hospitality units. The latter has its own access stair, jaunty styling and a generous circulation space capable of accommodating all kinds of gatherings.

The whole composition, the choice of materials and the fragmentation are intended to create an effect of lightness. The irregularly shaped roof is made of a material that offers protection against sun and rain while admitting light. It is suspended from an asymmetrically placed column and gives the stadium a distinctive silhouette when viewed from afar.

Spartastadion

name: Spartastadion
place: Rotterdam, the Netherlands
date of design: 1995
architects: UN Studio, Ben van Berkel and
Caroline Bos
capacity: 6,000 (pop concert);
soccer match: unknown

The old Sparta Stadium (1916) occupied a crucial site within Berlage's urban design plan for Rotterdam. Dubbed 'The Castle', it became the distinctive logo of the working-class district of Spangen. By the early 1990s, however, both the stadium and its environs were badly in need of refurbishment and it was decided to build a completely new sporting accommodation.

Ben van Berkel designed a multifunct-ional complex that eschews spectacular feats of engin-eering to transform the sports stadium into a con-cert venue or conference hall. Instead they opted for a strict separation between indoor and outdoor events by placing two differently sized bowls side by side and covering the smaller of the two. Together they form a building with a universal demeanour that would look perfectly at home in any one of a dozen metropolitan loca-tions. Soccer matches are played outside in the open air while the covered

section of the building accommodates pop concerts, festivals and small-scale sporting events. The open-air stadium has covered stands divided into eight sections, each with its own facilities aimed at specific tar-get groups. Where the two bowls meet, is a joint amenities block with rooms for VIPs, athletes and artists. In the event, the client decided not to build UN Studio's design but the plan put forward by Zwarts & Jansma for a stadium on the orig-inal site and incorpora-ting a distinctive element of the old stadium: the two towers that earned the stadium its nickname The Castle. The new Sparta Stadium opened its doors in 2000.

Dodger Stadium

name: Dodger Stadium
place: Los Angeles, United States
date of design: 1999
architects: Asymptote Architecture
(Hani Rashid & Lise Anne Couture Principals)
capacity: 75,000

The Dodger Stadium design has been used by Asymptote Architecture as a testing ground for a number of revolutionary technical innovations. The most important of these is the synthetic roof. The new materials of which it is composed not only afford protection against sun and rain but also allow the degree of transparency to be regulated by altering the air pressure in the pneumatic construction. In this way the penetration of light can be modulated during the day while at night full transparency allows television cameras hovering above the stadium to take pictures of the action below.

State of the art electronics provide the public with information about batting averages and a host of statistical details in both text and image. A vehicle mounted on rails and fitted out with a variety of public amenities rides around the circumference of the playing field, its tempo slow enough to allow people to step in and out of its shops and bars without difficulty. In this speculative project, Asymptote Architecture presents a visionary picture of a possible stadium of the future.

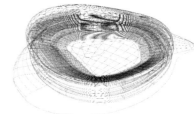

Interview with
Wiel Arets
'The stadium should be part of the city'

1   2

Wiel Arets set up his own architectural practice, Wiel Arets Architect & Associates, in 1984. He has held various visiting lectureships at universities and academies both at home and abroad. Since 1995 he has been Dean of the Berlage Institute in Amsterdam.

1-7. Provisional design for Euroborg Stadium in Groningen

What were your starting points in designing the stadium in Groningen?
Nearly all the stadia I know, certainly in the Netherlands, are built in the middle of a parking lot. The surrounding public space is often uninteresting. I remembered the square in Lucca (northern Italy) where an amphitheatre once stood. The city fell into disuse over the years but in the Middle Ages it was rebuilt in rings using materials from the amphitheatre. With Lucca as my example I conceived the idea of building a football stadium with another programme grouped around it. That other programme ensures that when there is no football scheduled there is enough programme left over to provide good public space in the surrounding area.

The design for Groningen consists of two elements. We made a building that includes a football stadium, and in addition to that we drew up a new spatial plan for the whole neighbourhood. We had a number of starting points: I've visited quite a few stadia and in Italy and Spain in particular they are located in residential areas. This works well and these stadia attract larger crowds than the Dutch ones. So one of my first concerns was not to place football outside society.

Secondly, I regarded the combination of different programmes as very important. When there is no football match or other big event, the hotel, cinema or other programme components should be able to use parts of the stadium.

This activity I call the 'hybrid programme'.

The final point is to ensure that a big structure like this is surrounded by good public space. People should be able to socialize here at any moment of the day. American stadia are usually located in parking lots on the outskirts of the city or in the middle of a tangle of freeways. That separation of functions does not fit in with Dutch tradition.

What is that Dutch tradition?

We like to have everything reasonably close together. We have good city centres were people work and live. The Dutch city has a hybrid programme compared with – to take the most extreme example – Brazilia, where all the programmes have been pulled apart and rationalized to death. I think a stadium can, by virtue of the way it is slotted into a city, have a positive effect on the social context.

Stadia are being allocated more and more leisure functions. How is that with this stadium?

It's absolutely true that leisure is a hot topic. You may ask yourself why. Human beings have discovered that there is more to life than work. As city dwellers we are pretty well obliged to work on our bodies once or twice a week and that means that leisure, free time and associated programmes are more than ever part of the modern city. But it's also interesting to see that sport helps to bring people together. In addition, sport accounts for a large part of the commer-

level. The roof becomes a park on which I can even locate programmes such as houses or a hotel. Raising that technological moment gives us the opportunity to develop other functions underneath. That is our greatest contrivance in my opinion.

For me architecture is everything relating to the concept of the building. I regard the up and down movement of that turf as architecture.

Could it be said that the stadium is the expression of cultural attitudes to sport?

For me a stadium is the expression of the city and the period in which we live. When you look at the façades of this stadium you don't see that there's a stadium behind it because it's become part of a complex. Renzo Piano's San Nicola stadium in Bari is very handsome but it is just a stadium. I didn't want to design a stadium for this site but an urban quarter with a place for the whole leisure business with sport and housing. That's a reversal of the basic principle. Sport is no longer relegated to the outskirts of the city. We've long since banned death from the city because we don't want to be confronted with deterioration but with eternal youth. Sport is a sort of incorporation of youth. It's interesting to notice that sport now has a very clear presence in our daily lives.

How do you think the stadium will develop in the future?

I think we'll abandon the notion of a football stadium on a parking lot on the outskirts of the city. In recent decades

3   4   5

cialization of society. Sport and leisure have become almost 'marketable' concepts and it is impossible to imagine the city without them.

I think the idea of a multi-purpose stadium is interesting but it mustn't be restricted to a single theme. A stadium must simply be a piece of the city, the way it used to be. Hence we have introduced a big housing complex into the stadium, as well as a hotel, a large cinema, entertainment facilities, shops and cafés. The stadium is surrounded by an attractive water feature and a lot of greenery. The roof will have grass and trees on it. The technical challenge of this stadium is the so-called lift-pitch. In some stadia the field slides out horizontally but for that you need an extra hectare of space next to the stadium. By raising the turf we kill three birds with one stone: in the first place the grass grows well, in the second place I can make the public space around the stadium perfect, but I can also use the roof as an extra

the programme of city centres has become increasingly one-sided because a lot of functions have been pushed to the urban periphery. In the development of the stadium you find that this typology is absorbing more and more programme. If the stadium becomes part of the city very different programmes will appear. That's what we're trying to show with the Groningen stadium. In addition, we are gradually living in a time when more and more things become invisible. We surround ourselves with equipment we often don't understand. Why should a stadium continue to be the visible physical expression of football? I don't think that matters at all. You used to be able to see that a building was a hospital or a school but that's not what we're about anymore. We develop new types of buildings in which various programmes find a place.

Cities are becoming increasingly interchangeable. What role does a stadium play in the development of an urban identity?

Quality of life is extremely important for a city nowadays. People have stopped going to businesses, businesses gravitate towards those cities where they think they will encounter the right people. But how do you go about making a good city? You do it by offering people a good house and public programme just round the corner. Every city needs a certain measure of urbanity. That's why I think the insertion of a stadium into the city, with as much programme as possible, is a major asset for Groningen. We thought hard and long about what the new city should be like and what we could add to Groningen to make it a more interesting city.

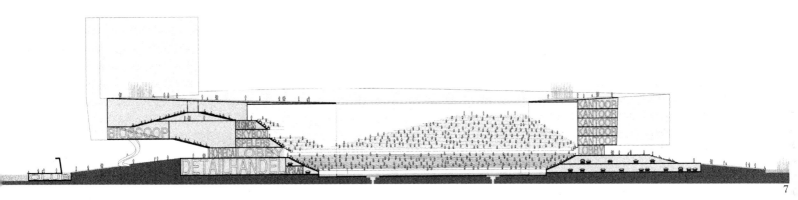

7

The favourite stadium of... *Jan Mulder*
sports journalist and ex-football player

'San Siro, before they put a roof on it. They have ruined it. The addition of roofs to those modern stadia has turned them into eyesores. You should be able to see a rim of little heads above the stands. What's wrong with a spot of rain during a football match? A short while ago, at a game in the Amsterdam ArenA, I heard someone say: "The roof was open because it wasn't raining." What nonsense! Football in the rain is great! People skate around in skimpy T-shirts these days, which is also ridiculous. What kind of world do we live in? And San Siro is a wonderfully proportioned rectangle. Arsenal has the most beautiful field, with great lines.'

Intervie

Ove Arup

'A stadium is more akin to a machin

In 1946 Ove Arup set up a private practice which concentrated on architectural engineering. The practice has grown exponentially since then and has offices in more than 50 countries.

What role does Ove Arup play in the design of stadia?
Bob Lang (associate director): We rarely design stadia on our own; we collaborate with architects, designers and contractors. A stadium is a highly engineered object, almost a machine for moving people in and out, providing technical facilities, allowing an event to take place. But equally there must be a certain level of art and poetry to it to make it a place that people enjoy. Often they are just exercises in extravagant design. To achieve a certain beauty and poetry, yet still achieving function, is a very precarious balance. We are creative collaborators. We are people who give advice on construction. But there are many disciplines that come into this: acoustics, lighting, calculating geometry, escape times for people to exits. We contribute the technology, as well as the more traditional things as heating, climatization, structure and of course foundations.

How will the stadium evolve in the future?
In classical architecture terms – the form and function argument – stadia are hugely functional places. There are strict rules of safety and organization and out of that rigour a certain

number of design options evolve. It is then down to the creativity of the team involved.

When you bring people very close to the pitch, which is what a good football stadium should, it is often at odds with other functions such as athletics or concerts. But people want to be close to the pitch, they want an intense atmosphere and in doing that of course the stands become very high, close and steep. That means it is difficult to get light onto the grass and to expose the pitch to the wind, all the natural ingredients that make a good playing surface. The space becomes restricted and the grass suffers. To take the pitch away and put it somewhere else for the majority of its life is therefore a very sensible thing to do. You merely pull the pitch in when you need it. Then you can ask the question what can you do with the space that is left?

What are the new technological trends?
We need to find ever more reliable ways of trying to encourage grass to grow in dark areas, or we take it outside the stadia. There is a lot of work to be done in terms of grass and turf technology. The same goes for acoustic control and daylight. Real advances need to be made in how we manipulate sound in the way that it emanates out of the stadium, especially in a residential area. Ever increasing mass is not a good thing to have on a very long span roof – the

w with

Partners
n to a classical building or structure'

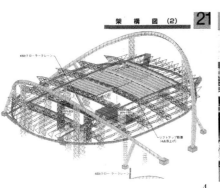

two things are diametrically opposed. So we need to think of how we solve the problem of acoustic control versus standing mass to the roof. The area of lighting as a whole is very interesting and of course there is always the conundrum between acoustic mass and light. Once you put mass in the roof, it is very difficult to get light through. A lightweight roof can allow a degree of natural daylight and won't make people feel repressed.

Also there are issues of adaptability of function. For example: just consider a stadium as a sports space and put athletics and football together. How do you bring the crowd close to the pitch for a football match and maybe next week move them far away to accommodate a running track? The two things again are diametrically opposed. There are technological advances to be made in moving large pieces of tribune or seating back and forth. Again that is more akin to a machine than to a classical building or structure.

Television is going to be a huge player in how much money is generated by the game. This influences stadium design, you need permanent camera positions for example. We ask the television consultants for advice right at the beginning of the design process to get strategic positions for the

1. Hartleyvale Stadium in Capetown, 1995

2. Hong Kong Stadium in Hong Kong, 1994

3-4. Ellis Park Stadium in Johannesburg, 1995

5-6. Lord's Mound Stand in London, 1987

cameras, and rails where mobile cameras can move. Is there any need for cameras in the roof, how many positions do you have, how do you get to those high level positions? Materials have made enormous advances over the twentieth century. Starting with steel, masonry and concrete, we've now got Teflon, PVC coatings, glass fibre and so on. These new materials make quite interesting geometric forms and can span long distances with low mass. This means vitality, lightness and excitement.

These new technologies lead to a project of theatre-like proportions. You need access for lighting, electricity, suspension points for major rigs, you need to be able to think about stage positions. Is it a theatre in the round, is it a focused-point stage, how many options do you give yourself? Is it a stadium that we've seen and understood for such a long time or is it a theatre?

What do you consider to be the urban impact of a stadium?
Stadia take enormous chunks of urban space. To put a major stadium in an out-of-town location means adding exit points to freeways, traffic control, roundabouts and huge infrastructure modifications. Then there is the question of

parking because for a short period of time, maybe twice a week, the whole car park is full and for the rest it becomes a huge desolate place. The large facilities in the States are on the edge of large cities and for the most part they are almost Cape Kennedy – a huge facility in the distance with a large space around it, as if it is a dangerous object, not to be approached.

It's not practical anymore to build stadia inside town, unless there is some reason of tradition, as with the new Wembley stadium for example. But the real urban impact is not the stadium itself, it is all the traffic and the congestion that it creates. The frequency of movement of people and the period between these large movements is a large difficulty to overcome. The first thing to look for when designing a stadium is a strategic location such as an intersection of motorways, railways or public transport. The process has to be turned around: first the location and connections and then the design for the stadium.

The Stade de France is considered to be an icon for regeneration. It has put an area of Paris on the map, but you could also have put something else there that would have served the same purpose, for example the Centre Pompidou. For a theatre or an art museum tends to attract a consistent, regular flow of people day by day; it becomes part of the fabric and that regular influx of people generates its own business and character. A stadium is a powerful injection of intense proportions but with very infrequent intervals and that leaves a space that is not so vibrant and not so pleasant. The design of the stadium is the fun bit. But there is a much bigger impact on the social fabric of a society when one of these things descends from above. We are very much aware of that.

There are two ways to approach the design of stadia. One is to create an architectural icon and then find a way of fitting the sport inside it; the other way is to consider what the stadium is there for and then find a roof, a structure and a form that suits what happens in stadia. Each way has its own advantages and disadvantages. Success is a blend of the two, because stadia are really hugely expressive forms and the structural performances required create interesting, dynamic forms.

Index

Colophon

Published on the occasion of the exhibition 'The Stadium. The Architecture of Mass Sport', held at the Netherlands Architecture Institute in Rotterdam from 8 June to 23 September 2000.

With the assistance of the team who prepared the exhibition:
Matthijs Bouw; Lilet Breddels; Iris Diederich; Ewout Dorman; Ernst van der Hoeven; Fransje Hooimeijer; Kristin von Nitzsch; Winnie Poon; Annuska Pronkhorst; Marieke van Rooij; Annet Tijhuis; Bas Vogelpoel

With thanks to the exhibition's sponsors:
Gemeente Rotterdam – Projectbureau Rotterdam EK 2000; Hoogovens; HunterDouglas; Ministerie van OC&W; Stichting VSB Fonds; Ontwikkelings-bedrijf Rotterdam; Stadion Feyenoord; ENECO; Volker Wessels Vastgoed; Multi Vastgoed; HBG; Mediamax Group; Ruijgrok (De Stier) Hekwerk; Hollandia; HOK + LOBB London; EDG Visual Communications; De Schelde Internationaal; Heras Hekwerk

Catalogue:
Concept and editing: Michelle Provoost
Design: Via Vermeulen / Rick Vermeulen and Natascha Frensch
Translation: Robyn de Jong-Dalziel; Andrew May
(Foreword, Van Rooy, Favourite Stadium)
Picture research: Fransje Hooimeijer, Ernst van der Hoeven
Lithography and printing: Drukkerij Snoeck-Ducaju & Zoon, Ghent
Production: Barbera van Kooij
Publisher: Simon Franke

Photography:
Cover Paul van Riel
ABC Press 56; Aerofilms Limited 80, 81; Alynia 152, 153; ANP 13, 16, 87; Marcel Antonisse (ANP) 120; Wiel Arets 132, 175, 176, 177; Ove Arup & Associates 136, 178, 179; Asymptote Architecture 174; Ballast Nedam Utiliteitsbouw 126, 151; G. Senad Becanin 89-91; Berenco Gardin 139; Berg Arkitektkontor 128; Nicolas Borel 35, 113, 130; Bundesarchiv Koblenz 65; Decq & Benoît 172; Dienst R.O. Amsterdam 129; Roger Dohmen (ANP) 86; Peter Eisenman 171; Ellerbe Becket 74, 75, 76; Georges Fessy 105, 106; Martin Gerlach 20, 24, 25; Mick Hales 134; Hans Heus 84, 85, 118, 119, 120, 121; HNTB 70, 71, 72; Gemeentearchief Rotterdam 115; Hulton Getty 14, 15; Göksin Sipahiolu (ABC press) 84; Gregotti Associati 108, 109, 133; Kurt Grimm 20; Hariu + Abe Cooperative Atelier 168; Hiroshi Hara + Atelier 169; HOK Sports Facilities Group 101, 102, 103, 110, 111, 131; Images Press 55; Fris Imatge 135; Simon Inglish 32, 47, 68; Institut für Stadtgeschichte Frankfurt/Main 20; IOC/Olympic Museum Collections 21, 22; S. Ishida 139; HOK + LOBB 48, 49, 50, 132; Christian Kandzia 65; Keystone – Sygma (ABC press) 86; Kenji Kobayashi 155; Leon Krige 178; Kisho Kurokawa 52, 53; Landesbildstelle Berlin 29; Marceau Lepinay 133; Duccio Malagamba 61; MBM Arquitectes 135; Morphosis 170; Osamu Murai 95; Novosti/V. Vyatkin 55; Tomio Ohashi 53; Ronald Ophuis 119; John de Pater 57, 166; Senad Pecanin 89, 90, 91; Hayo Piebenga 115; RAN International Architects & Engineers 54, 56, 57, 127, 157; Leni Riefenstahl 19, 30, 28; Rivero (ANP) 119; Charlotte Rohrbach (Ullstein Bilderdienst) 26, 27, 30, 78, 79; Marieke van Rooij 123, 133; Takenaka Corperation 116; Thijs Tummers 29, 39, 43, 45, 82, 83, 92, 97, 99, 104, 109, 110, 115, 131, 140, 141, 149; Kajima Corporation 164, 165; Toshiharu Kitajima 117, 155; UN Studio 173; V G Bild-Kunst 158/159; Ari Versluis & Ellie Uyttenbroek 158/159; Voermans van Bree 153; Zwarts & Jansma 114, 144, 145, 146, 150, 151

It was not possible to find all the copyright holders of the illustrations used. Interested parties are requested to contact NAi Publishers, Mauritsweg 23, 3012 JR Rotterdam, The Netherlands.

Available in North, South and Central America through D.A.P./Distributed Art Publishers Inc, 155 Sixth Avenue 2nd Floor, New York, NY 10013-1507, Tel. 212 627.1999 Fax 212 627.9484

Available in the United Kingdom and Ireland through Art Data, 12 Bell Industrial Estate, 50 Cunnington Street, London W4 5HB, Tel. 181-747 1061 Fax 181-742 2319

Printed and bound in Belgium

ISBN 90-5662-145-9